D1613107

The World is full of Charlies

Down in the Jungle

It's very plain to see

"The World is Full of Charlie's

as well as me!"

[signature]

The World is full of Charlies

Recollections of a lifetime in show business by

Charlie Chester

NEW ENGLISH LIBRARY
TIMES MIRROR

Dedicated to a variety of people who have helped me enjoy a full life with the people of variety – and especially my family who saw me occasionally.

CHAPTER ONE

We may not see the
whole of the way – but
we can always take the first step.

THERE is no such thing as a straight line between the cradle
and the grave. It's a series of ups and downs, and twists
and turns, pleasures and heartaches, and one positive way
of realising this is to take up show business as a career.

Breaking into show business is about as funny as an
armpit with a boil, at least it was, back in the thirties. I won
countless talent competitions, singing and yodelling with
my guitar, aping an American singer called Jimmie Rogers,
and it was after winning the All South London Winners
Competition at Camberwell Palace that I gave an audition
to Jack De Freece – as a comic.

I have never been so nervous since the day I first shook
hands with a real theatrical agent, and I know I was scared

then that he would want to deduct one finger for his commission.

Praying that the frayed strings on my ukelele would survive my act I remember how vast the stage seemed to be, then from the black void in front of me, a voice boomed out: "Well get on with it."

I went through my routine with about as much confidence as Crippen must have had when he stood on the gallows, and when I had finished the voice came across the auditorium again: "OK. That'll do. Now go away and learn to shave and you'll be a good comic one day!"

I thought that it was a fatuous remark to make, but I have long since realised that there was a great deal of wisdom in what he said. I made the mistake of cracking jokes about the wife and the girl friend in the same breath. I was too young to have a wife, and sounded like a dirty young boy. By the same standards, if I'd cracked gags about the wife and the girl friend too late in life, I would have sounded like a dirty old man.

The fact that I had a very close facial resemblance to a man named Harry Sargeant of Brighton, coupled with the fact that I too had a similar Sussex accent (I was born in Tideswell Road, Eastbourne), was something of an added drawback, for apart from looking like him it also "sounded" as if I was copying him. Harry objected to my act and as a result I was barred for about nine years from playing the great Moss Empires.

Harry Sargeant better known as Max Miller – was just about the greatest front-cloth comic ever, and I am certain he was not in any danger of my knocking him off his great pedestal. Yet it was a consolation to me to know that if I worried him enough to have me kept off the Moss tours, I must have *something* at least. After that I purposely stayed away from watching him perform in case I inadvertently adopted any of his mannerisms. But years later, Max and I shared top of the bill together, and after his death, I was asked to play Max Miller in the film, *Stars of Music*

Hall, and sing *Mary from the Dairy*, a song not about a farm girl, as one might imagine, but about a waitress called Mary in the Express Dairy at the bottom of Charing Cross Road.

Of course, looking back on the very early days of one's career brings many a laugh, many a shudder, and many a sigh, and although I can't remember who said it, full marks to the one who said: "What a pity that youth is wasted on children. If only we could be twenty-one again and know what we know today."

I often say I'd do it all over again, and yet, sometimes I have second thoughts.

I remember for instance, after knocking around with a concert party gaining experience, having played with Dixies Dance Band in Ewell in Surrey (guitar and vocals) and even having my own accordion band when I was about 17, I decided that I could make more money as a single act. I played one-night stands, clubs, masonics and so on, working under the name of Duke Daly. It was twelve shillings and sixpence for the act and two and six extra if you were called back for an encore. The embarrassing part of it was that the entertainments manager would stand in a small partitioned section of the stage listening to the applause, and after taking a couple of calls I had to wait, eyeball to eyeball, for him to nod or shake his head.

I was "discovered" by a popular band leader at about this time. His name was Ben Oakley, a big strong man who seemed to like my style. On one particular night I had to play a golf club at Hendon, then go on to the police annual dance at Edgware and from there to Lewisham.

I did so well at the golf club that I had to do much longer than I had anticipated. It was then a toss up between the other two dates as I couldn't possibly manage both. After tossing a coin Edgware won and I phoned Harold Collins, the leader of the pit orchestra at Lewisham Hippodrome, and explained that I couldn't make his date and fortunately he understood. It was at the Edgware Police

Dance that Ben Oakley and his band were playing. I went through my routine and after the show Ben asked me if I would do a cabaret for him at the Thatched Barn near Boreham Wood. I said I would and it was then that he introduced me to a man named Reg Morgan, who was once John McCormack's pianist. "He knows everybody," said Ben, "and he'd like to manage you." And so he did until the outbreak of war.

The date at the Thatched Barn, however, was agreed and when I arrived Ben gave me my instructions. "It's a mixed do Charlie, but don't let that worry you, give it to 'em strong son."

"Not full out surely? I mean, there are ladies present."

"The lot, Charlie. I'm paying you and I'm telling you it's OK."

I kept to my instructions and began my sauciest routine and while I was working on the floor a half drunk kept walking in front of me and each time he passed he muttered: "Clear off, or I'll do you!"

When I finished my act Ben asked me what was wrong with me. I told him that the drunk kept saying I was going to get "done". Ben noticed that the man was hovering near the door, so he excused himself and went to the front entrance and then came back in and told the fellow that he was wanted on the phone. I saw the man follow Ben out and shortly afterwards Ben returned and settled up with me saying: "It's OK now Duke, he won't bother you." I left almost immediately and just outside, hung up on the railings by his coat collar, looking for all the world like a scarecrow, was the drunk. Ben had knocked him out cold.

*

The Blue Hall Islington was the place where up and coming performers were booked at a fee of about thirty shillings and it was where theatrical agents went to scout for talent.

It was there that I saw an old music hall comic called Jack Warman fighting to get laughs and only got them when he had a coughing fit, or sneezed, and his false teeth flew out.

Teeth, especially false teeth, are not exactly pretty things out of their proper environment and once, just before he was due on stage, Frank Randle, the Northern favourite, suddenly whipped round to me and said: "Hold these for me Charlie," and there, in my hand were his choppers. I shuddered and was glad to hand them to the stage manager.

Teeth were the subject of another joke when the irrepressible Crazy Gang pulled one on Charlie Naughton at the Vaudeville Golfing Society Dinner. This is a pros' do where anything goes, it's naughty and it's fun. Charlie was sitting next to me and at the other side of him was Jimmy Nervo, of Nervo and Knox.

It was approaching coffee time and speeches were about to begin when suddenly someone pulled a string opening a box full of plaster which had been carefully placed directly above where Charlie Naughton sat.

"Christ, the bloody ceiling's fell in!" he said. After the commotion settled down we were brought fresh coffee cups, large ones. I never saw Jimmy Nervo do it, but as Charlie drank his coffee, and slowly the cup emptied a full set of somebody's teeth were revealed at the bottom. Charlie turned green. I wasn't surprised.

The ups and downs of show business are only a part of my story, and just as vivid in my mind are the embarrassments of "growing up".

My father, who was a brilliant painter and artist, had his own sign-writing business in Eastbourne. He was known as the fastest sign writer on the South Coast through being the first with the idea of spray painting. He obtained a tank from an airship which landed on Beachy Head during the First World War, and my elder brother George and I used to have to pump this up to pressure of 120 lb. My father then used to cut out stencils which he pinned to the poster,

11

things such as Charlie Chaplin's silhouette, for the local cinema to advertise films such as *The Kid*. Another cut-out I remember was a bulldog for *Bulldog Drummond*, and so on. He would then spray the Argonaut dye from a small chromium instrument, like an oversized fountain pen with a small cup on it, which contained the dye. After spraying the cut-out, it was then removed and the figure and the writing were perfect. This was repeated as many times as the poster was required, and to have done the same thing in actual sign writing would have taken considerably longer.

Unfortunately, my dad was a heavy drinker, and he loved women. He was also a fine figure skater and enjoyed a part-time job as a roller skating instructor at Devonshire Park. I vaguely remember it being said that he was one of the few exponents of the "madman's leap", but I never discovered what it was.

Somehow he managed to wade through a fortune and finally left Eastbourne to come to London. So for a while my brother and I had to stay with my grandmother at the Lodge Inn, which was a single line of bungalows situated on the Crumbles not far from where a particularly sordid murder took place.

Later, when George and I went to London to join our parents we were met at Victoria Station and I remember seeing my father, for the first time ever, down at heel, a tired and dejected man. The sadness of that moment will never leave me.

I was always proud of my father as most kids are, and yet sad to relate, he never had any time for me. I was his big disappointment in life, he had wanted a girl. I can only remember him taking me out a few times. Once or twice to see Charlie Chaplin and on another occasion for a picnic on Beachy Head, when he took off his belt, hooked it through his walking stick, and allowed my brother and I to hold on to the cane whilst he ran down the hill, pulling us both behind him. It was fun, but even that didn't last long – I fell in a cow pat on the way down.

As far as my father's drinking habits were concerned, suffice it to say that he was drunk more times than I can remember, and seldom spoke to me. He even stole the rent money on one occasion to pay for drink, and the rows were constant.

Notwithstanding all this, I am sure they were very much in love with each other for she always forgave him and he called her "dreamer" which was short for Beautiful Dreamer.

It is extraordinary how a single event can completely change the course of a man's life; for my brother George the change of course came when he took a job as a milkman. He was late for work one morning and he borrowed an old bicycle that had stood, unused for years behind the front door. It belonged to the people in the basement. George thought that if he borrowed it to get to work on time, he could return it before anyone noticed its disappearance. Unfortunately someone did notice and poor brother George was accused of stealing it.

When my father returned home from work, the row was still in evidence, and the outcome was that he hit my brother so hard that the blood spattered all over the ceiling. My brother, covered in blood, had to go and apologise to Mrs Mitchell. When she saw him she fainted.

The following day, when George came home from work he told me: "That's it Tich. He won't do that to me again; I've taken the King's Shilling." He went away to serve seven years in the Beds and Herts Regiment. It was a bitter blow to my father because George was his pride and joy.

If I give the impression that my father was some sort of ogre or bully I am doing him an injustice. He was strict but the incident over the bicycle was the only occasion he hit George. He was painstakingly aware of our manners towards our elders – a personality trait which, I like to believe, paid dividends for me later in life. But what hurt me more than anything else was his lack of communication. He also made George and I fear him. For example, when my brother had been playing with the fire, my father tried to teach him a lesson

13

by putting the poker in the fire until it was red hot and, with my brother screaming under the table, he held it to within an inch of his leg, just to make him realise that fire was dangerous and would hurt.

I can only remember him hitting me once (I do not classify incidentally, a smack across the backside as being hit), and I received a black eye for losing a pound note; not surprising in those days when a pound was worth a pound.

Just as many men can be the life and soul of the public houses, when my father came home, it was like a cloud descending over the house; he was morose and seldom spoke. In the pub he would joke, play his accordion for hours on end and buy "drinks all round" and yet when he came home and walked into a room, I went out of it. It was because of his drinking that I was a teetotaller until I was over forty. I hated him for it, not realising that it was not entirely his fault. Circumstances in those days were enough to drive any family man to drink though some were stronger than others. I don't suppose my yodelling and guitar playing helped his temperament (hardly the cure for a hangover). I used to practise in the passageway at the back of the house, which, because of its concrete floor, created an echo.

I heard my father say: "If he wants to make that bloody noise, tell him to go into his bedroom."

I did. Ironically enough I was rehearsing a song for a competition, called *My Old Pal*. It went like this:

> I am dreaming tonight of an old Southern Town
> and the best pal that I ever had.
> For I've grown so weary of roaming around
> I'm going back home, to my Dad.
> Your hair has turned to silver
> I know you're fading too
> Daddy, dear old Daddy . . . ee
> I'm coming back to you

14

You made my boyhood happy, but still I longed to
   roam
I've had my way, but now I'll stay
I long for you and for home.

There might have been something Freudian about the
song because I was a total introvert when my father was at
home.

But my mother and I used to laugh like drains when we
were alone. She loved a naughty joke. I called her my
Daisy – but as soon as we heard the front door slam,
it was, "Here comes your father!" and silence reigned.

When later I turned to comedy and had developed a
routine, my father often had a party at the house for his
boozing pals. I would be asked to play the piano and sing
my new comedy songs. But I just couldn't do it. This offended and annoyed him. He wanted to show me off on the
one hand amusing his pals, and yet when I practised, it
bothered him. It was sad in a way that we only became
friendly after I left home and for two years before he died
my father and I were the greatest of pals.

*

My early encounters with the girls weren't all they might
have been.

I used to go to a cafe in Clapham to meet a waitress
called Olwen. I took her out a few times to the cinema but
the relationship progressed no further.

Then I received a letter from her mother in Wales saying:
"I am so pleased to hear from Olwen that you are going to
marry her, due to the fact that she is going to have a
baby." I dropped her like a hot coal. It obviously wasn't
mine, and the fact that she had gone that far with someone
else deterred me from further involvement.

For a while I changed my hobbies and busied myself

entering talent competitions and running my amateur band. It was about this time I fancied myself as a poet, and innocently I boasted of my talent to a young woman who came with us on one of our Sunday outings. I confess I was totally besotted by the woman (I'll call her Wanda here, but that was not her name) and when she asked me if I could write a poem on any subject I told her I could.

"All right," she said. "Supposing a mother had lost her baby, would that make a good poem?" I confidently replied that it would and I would have it for her next time we met.

I remember sitting up half the night drawing cherubs round the edge of the paper to frame the masterpiece and, later, when the tears that rolled down Wanda's lovely face as she read it under a lamplight in Hyde Park, I felt about as powerful as any man could. She swore it was the loveliest poem she had ever read and added that she would keep it for ever.

Some weeks later, when my mother noticed the shine on my well-worn shoes, she asked me where I was going.

"To see Wanda," I replied a little bashfully.

"Have a good time. Is she a nice girl?"

"Super. She's coming with me to Camberwell Empire for the talent competition."

But when I arrived home, there was a distinct chill in the air and my mother asked: "Where have you been?"

"I told you. Out with Wanda."

"Aren't you ashamed of yourself?"

"No, why should I be? I won the competition, and then took Wanda home!"

"Never mind the competition. *I'm* talking about this girl. I'm ashamed of you!"

I was mystified. And then my mother went on. "Well, while you've been out with her, your father's been trying to square things with her husband – to stop you being named as the co-respondent in a divorce case!"

"What do you mean?"

16

"Oh now don't play the innocent with me son. You *knew* she was married, didn't you?"

"Married?"

"Don't lie. You knew she was married. You knew that she had had a baby and lost it, because her husband found the poem you wrote about it in her handbag."

I remember being terrified of what the outcome would be because Wanda's husband was, I discovered later, a detective inspector at Scotland Yard.

I never saw Wanda again. "I will not harbour vice. It would be better if you left," my mother told me. So with heavy heart I packed a bag and although at the door she said she didn't mean it I left home.

Regardless of this my Daisy-Mum (I continued to call her Daisy-Mum) and I were the greatest of pals until she died. I don't think she ever quite believed that I didn't know Wanda was married but with that poem as evidence against me I couldn't really blame her.

*

When I turned full pro, my dates were handed over to a club comic whom I have never met to this day. He had a reputation for being a good act and I asked him on the phone if he would undertake all my existing club dates. His name was Klifton Court of Brixton.

I asked him to take over because I wanted to start afresh as a pro with Reg Morgan as my manager, who was also handling a singer called Robert Ashley. I was then taken to an agent in Piccadilly named Michael Mitchell, whose name belied the fact that he was of Polish origin and spoke English with a thick gutteral accent. The fact that his English wasn't so good didn't help me much. I was expected to stand in front of his desk and do my fast-talking patter routine to him alone, while Reg sat in a corner and waited. Can you imagine it? An audience of *one* sitting behind a desk and practically a foreigner at that ...?

"Good evening, ladies and gentlemen, I was standing in the pub a minute ago and a young girl came in and stood next to me. I said 'Hello love are you going to have one?' She said: 'No, it's just the way me coat's buttoned!'"

Silence. I could almost hear the beads of sweat dropping from my face to the floor.

With managerial loyalty Reg would laugh at every gag, but then with a sepulchral voice the agent would look at him and say "Zo . . . iss dat funny?"

The balm to the humiliation was that I was booked for Romano's, The Bristol Grill and the Piccadilly Hotel, where I died on my feet twice nightly. I almost longed to go back to the clubs. I was both glad and sorry when I was retained for a further three weeks.

I think the Piccadilly Hotel was the worst. I had to work upstairs in the restaurant for one show and it was like a morgue. No one laughed and you felt that you were intruding on their privacy.

Downstairs was different. This was the grill, and while you stood on the floor doing a comedy routine of patter, the waiters would be flying past you this way and that, together with the rattling of the knives and forks. The whole affair was a bedlam of noise.

The only night-club I really made a hit at was Quaglino's. It was only a one-night stand, but when the great American raconteur Fred Duprez died suddenly, I was sent to fill the bill. At the end of my act, they barred my exit from the floor and called for more so many times I actually ran out of material.

My first actual theatre engagement in variety was for George Barclay, the husband of the famous Kate Carney. Jack was a small man who owned the Alexandria in Stoke Newington.

My act went down so well there that I was retained for a further two weeks and offered yet another. I turned the last offer down though, saying that I'd rather not wear out my welcome. The truth was I didn't have enough material to keep the act fresh.

Variety was in its hey day, with acts like Billy Bennett, Will Hay, Forsythe, Seaman and Farrell, The Royal Elliots, Billy Russell, Max Miller, Ted Ray, Tommy Trinder and so on. There were so many fine performers to choose from that dates for newcomers were scarce.

In my case, the bar went up because I resembled Miller, so there was only Stoll tours, which was five variety halls, and the independent dates for me to play, if, and when, they wanted me.

I remember sitting on the embankment with Teddy Formby, George's younger brother (who still writes to me to this day), when we felt very unwanted and found solace in each other's plight. It was twopence all the way on the tram from Blackfriars to Clapham before four o'clock, and so I had the choice of going by tram, or hanging on the back of a lorry and buying half a pound of apples for lunch with the money instead.

On one occasion I was so fed up I rang Moss Empires and spoke to Val Parnell, the boss under old George Black. I said: "Mr Parnell, this is Charlie Chester, look, I'm a young man and I want to work!"

"Well buy yourself a pick and shovel!" came the reply. That piece of advice cost me the only twopence I possessed in the world!

Many years later, when I occupied the Number One dressing room at the London Palladium, I toyed with the idea of having a silver pick and shovel crest made so that I could pin it to the door and invite Mr Parnell to see it. I could imagine myself saying: "I bought that bloody pick and shovel, it's hanging on my door." But George and Alfred Black, two wonderful men who I was contracted to for ten years, had beaten me to it: they had a brass Charlie Chester nameplate there instead. It adorns the door of my den at home, and is one of the things I treasure.

I suppose there is a well of hope in all of us, and I recall that out of the blue, after waiting for a long time, I obtained a contract to appear and share top of the bill at the Colliseum, Portsmouth with Eric Randolph, whose billing was Paulo, the singing clown. The only other act on the bill I remember was Billy Whittaker and Mimi, a wonderful pair of companions.

My weekly salary then was twenty-seven pounds ten shillings. Being the independent small date we had to do a matinee, so the people from the Moss theatre, the Hippodrome, would come in. To my surprise I had a visit from the top of the bill of the opposition, which was Horace Golding, the famous magician. He arrived with his wife at my dressing room and told me that he liked my act and would I like to work for him. It was manna from Heaven.

"What are you asking for the act?" he asked.

"Well, I'm getting twenty-seven ten," I said rather proudly.

"I can offer you twenty-two ten," he said, "and I can offer you two years work."

Suddenly it came to me.

Two years work and some of it at the big Moss Empires. I was made. In those days it was nothing short of a miracle. With that money I could see myself saving a fortune.

"I'll sign," I said with alacrity.

He smiled and reached into his pocket and brought out the contract – already made out. I signed my name and I had wings on my heart.

Security at last.

Horace Golding dropped dead the following week at Wood Green Empire after doing his famous bullet trick. I was back to square one. No dates. No money, and I was still barred by Moss Empires.

Although in the early days I was a nonentity, Reg Morgan introduced me to the Ascot Club in Charing Cross Road. This was the haunt of all the greats of show biz and (though why, I'll never know) they accepted me from the word go.

It's true that I had done a few broadcasts and had worked for five months at the Prince of Wales Theatre in Piccadilly in Alfred Esdailes *Frivolities de France*.

I was second comic to Naunton Wayne and therefore not much of a force to be reckoned with. The show was a nude non-stop revue, and if I had never seen a naked girl till I was eighteen, I certainly made up for it then.

The girls were used to it though. They were less aware of their nudity than we were, but after a while, even we got used to it and it would be a simple friendly gesture to squeeze a pert bosom when passing a girl talking on the phone backstage.

Fun was the predominant thought, and I recall that in one sketch I had to be the lover who hid in the wardrobe. I had to remain there quietly through practically the whole of the sketch.

On one occasion I found this almost an impossibility, for the male part of a dancing team from Australia, called Latasha and Lawrence, had bored a hole without my knowing in the back of the wardrobe, and in one performance I had the best part of half a hat pin rammed into my backside!

I was still very new to the profession and was a bag of nerves each time I went on. It was in a sketch called *Goddess of the Golden Jungle* that I suffered the terrible experience of drying up. The scene involved a rather nice, hard, Amazon girl who had to be naked and painted gold. The law was that she could be naked if she didn't move.

At the end of the scene she ran off, covered in the wet paint, to go straight to the bath and we all made way for her.

On this occasion, I was standing outside the two swing doors which led to the stage and as she barged through she knocked the head of my ukelele, and although I didn't know it at the time, the string heads had been dislodged and loosened all the strings.

I ran like hell to get on stage realising I was late and there was a "stage wait". I arrived in the centre of the stage out of breath, not the best way to sing a song – and when I went to strum my uke . . . nothing. The strings made no sound, they were all loose, and at that moment, little George Beaumont, the musical director in the pit, looked up and whispered "Your flies are undone!" It was one of the few occasions I was stuck for words.

You can only buy experience with time, and by listening to people who have experience. That's why I enjoyed being welcomed into the Ascot Club. Will Fyffe, Will Hay, Billy Bennett, Dusty Rhodes, Sam Mayo, The Crazy Gang, Al Bowley, Harry Hemsley, Charlie Austen, they were all there and many others. Many is the time I had an arm around my shoulder and heard a remark like: "Stick at it little Charlie, it'll come, you'll see."

Charlie Austen even asked me to write his sketches for him when he did an act called "Do you want to be an actor?"

Will Fyffe took me aside one day, and said to me. "You want to stick to radio Charlie, that's your forte." And after all the years I've been doing radio I have a feeling that he wasn't far wrong.

Talking about Will Fyffe, don't let anyone kid you that all Scotsmen are mean. I remember that any out-of-work actor at that time could always get a free steak and kidney pudding dinner on Friday and it was always paid for by Will. It was a generous gesture, and one that I would often liked to have accepted, but I was too proud.

As time went by, I began to wonder when I would be offered a Moss date, but still the bar was in force. Max Miller even came to the Prince of Wales with a solicitor, to see if there were any way to stop me working. There wasn't. I was using my own material, such as it was, and had my own personality. By now I had lost my Sussex accent and was being accepted as a cockney.

Then I was offered the lead in a show written by Bruce Sevier called *Silly Isn't It*? The music was by Hans May (the writer of such marvellous music as *Starlight Serenade* and many others). Hans was a small gentle little Viennese and a typical composer.

The producer was a Henry Saltenburg, a Prussian, and the dominance of Mr Saltenburg over Hans caused many a furious argument, which were really very funny to listen to.

Saltenburg: "Come on then. Gif to me a Ra ta ta ta."

Hans: "But dere iss no Ra ta ta ta."

Saltenburg (banging everything in sight): "But I *must hef a* Ra ta ta ta.

The show was really a concocted version of *Charley's Aunt*, only there were three Aunts – all played by me. I never stopped changing in that show and was a ball of sweat from start to finish.

Thank God it only represented the second half of the show, the first half being variety.

The girls were the Rodney Hudson girls, and their captain was a Dorita Langley. She felt so sorry for me that every interval she brought me a cup of tea. I have been drinking her tea ever since – we married in 1939.

During the run of this show, which only lasted a week, I wanted to repay the girls for their kind thought, and I offered to run them back to Victoria from Bromley in my car, a Ford V 8.

This was my third car and none of them had brought me much joy. The first was a second-hand Austin, which broke down in Chatham after I had a row with the management of the Theatre Royal. My billing outside the theatre could have been hidden with a knife edge and I wasn't pleased. Bebe Daniels and Ben Lyon were in their proper place at the top of the bill, with forty-eight of their photos outside, and I felt it was only fair to include at least one of mine. The result was the management and I agreed to cancel the contract.

Then the car broke down and after I had been towed back to Lewisham where I had bought it on the "never", the salesman said, "What you really need is a more solid car. Now it's a few pounds more, but here's a Standard. It's far from new, but it's a solid job. Three gears only, this is more the car for you.''

I signed the documents and drove out across Lewisham High Street – and the door fell off. After another wrangle with the car man, he agreed that a more modern car was what I really needed. Yes, the Ford V 8 was the job for me, nothing wrong with it except that the battery was down a bit.

This was the Ford V 8 in which I offered to take the girls back to Victoria. I was glad to be able to repay their kindness, and as I cranked up with the starting handle it flew back and dislocated my wrist. Dorita sat up front with me, trying to work the joint back into position. It was a terrible journey. It was the end of yet another show and, for me, the start of a new era.

Travel wisely, travel safely . . . and it does help if you know where you are going.

CHAPTER TWO

Take an example from the best,
learn a lesson from the worst,
and you've won a first degree
in living.

VARIETY, or music hall, was a way of life; hectic and
enjoyable. Weeks out of work and weeks of sheer apprehension. The act went well at Luton, but would it do the
same at Didsbury? I wonder who will be on the bill with us?
Is there a good "drawing" name at the top of the bill?
And what will the digs be like?

Living in a suitcase is something you get used to. Living
with your brother and sister artistes you become almost like
a family. It's not long before you know each other's pedigree
and background. Most of the old performers became so
much like brothers that they founded an order called The
Grand Order of Water Rats.

I will tell you more about this in a later chapter.

The strength and importance of show business has always been the "names" of the people in it, and the backbone of their existence has been divided up into categories: variety; revue; plays; summer season; pantomime; cabaret; films; musicals and so on.

Alas, pantomime, the show-biz world of makebelieve for kids, which was a must for every town and every city, is fast becoming a thing of the past. How many great names have been at their greatest when donning the "skirts" to play Dame? People with the artistry of Freddie Forbes, Norman Evans, Clarkson Rose, Arthur Askey and Arthur Lucan (Old Mother Riley) to name but a few.

When I first went into pantomime for Emile Littler, the great impresario, I played the same character, in the same panto, for several consecutive years. I was supposed to be Simple Simon. We found, however, that by now, my own name of Cheerful Charlie was bigger than that of the character, so I was called simply Cheerful Charlie. I was the village idiot (type casting of course).

With me, and playing his first pantomime, was one of the most brilliant minds in the business. A very lovable and educated gentleman with a boyish approach to everything. He loved noise, and gags that went "bang". He was crazy, he was great, he played Mr Twist, the crooked man in *Jack and Jill* at the Casino in London. His name was Michael Bentine.

Michael had, some time before, taken London by storm with his chair back routine and was ideal for the part. But half way through the show he was depressed, and Emile was constantly sending notes around about one's performance.

He said to me one day: "You see, Chas, it's all right for you. You've got it!"

"Got what?" I asked.

"The sympathy, they love you. They hate me because I'm the wicked Uncle."

26

"Well, you don't have to be the wicked uncle. Play it as an eccentric uncle, or even a lovable uncle. Play for sympathy."

"Wouldn't it worry you if I played it for sympathy?" he asked.

"Play it any way you want, it makes no difference."

Before I explain how he played it I must point out that pantomimes survive a long run after the kids have gone back to school because of the old-age pensioner clubs, The Silver Strands, The Darby and Joans and so on. One had only to give them a mention from the stage and you were virtually guaranteed a round of applause.

Mike walked on, wishing to kill the image of a wicked uncle, and as he roared his words out in a mad-professor type of delivery, a child started to cry.

Michael looked down with a hurt expression. "Ah, what a shame," he said, with due concern. "Madam, I'll tell you how you can stop that. Open the little darling's mouth and pour in a pound and a half of molten lead!"

They froze on him.

I fell about with hysterical laughter. So this was playing it for *sympathy*?

Michael realised that all was not well and like the real pro his mind was quickly working his way out of it. He suddenly remembered the Darby and Joan get out.

"Ah," he said hurriedly. "It's nice to see that we have the Darby and Joan Clubs with us, and it's rather strange, but you see that table there (he pointed to a prop table which collapsed while he was talking about it). That was made to last forever. It was made in the days of William the Conqueror . . . (pause to look around). You all remember William the Conqueror?" (another pause to search their faces) then . . . "Some of you must have *known him!*"

Poor Michael he came off sweating profusely to find us all in hysterics. At least he had a good audience back stage.

27

It was in that same show I had my instructions to play for sympathy and to this end I had to work with a tiny young girl who played Mary, Mary, and also do some song and dance routines with the Terry Juveniles.

With my specially designed tall hat and costume, I looked very tall alongside these young maidens of the theatre.

The particular song and routine I shall never forget was *Zing Zing Zing a Little Song With Me*; I bend double every time I think of it.

As I sang the words, the twelve little girls split into two sections and played tug o' war with me, pulling me this way and that. At the end of the routine there was a most effective finish. I stood on one leg with my arms both pushed out in front of me, the girls then aligned themselves alongside me and with a concerted heave they lifted me bodily, high over their heads and danced rhythmically off stage.

It looked like a feat of strength, although actually it was quite easy for them. But one night a hand from the forest of dainty digits holding me high was hanging on for dear life to my testicles. Prostrate above their heads I could do nothing but sweat. She clung very tightly and I swear that at one time she was lifted off the floor.

When they finally put me down back stage, I looked around them for a guilty face, but all I saw was a ring of angelic faces, but one of those little perishers almost tore my medals off.

Emile Littler had very set ideas on how his pantomimes should run. Strictly script. Family humour and keep to the character. He even made me wear a blond bubble-cut wig to fit the character I was playing.

Johnny Lockwood, the knockabout comic, was once playing Buttons in *Cinderella* for him, and during rehearsals Johnny said: "Well goodbye Cinders, I'll see you later," and so saying he did a very funny back flip and prat fall.

28

Emile stormed down to the front. "What the hell do you think you're doing?" he asked.

Still on the floor, Johnny replied. "I was just making a funny exit."

"Well I don't want it, we all know that you're an acrobat. You're supposed to be Buttons. Any acrobatics and it's like saying 'I can speak Spanish!' "

Johnny looked puzzled, apologised and carried on.

A few days later he did the same thing again. He suddenly realised that he shouldn't have done it and lying full length on the stage, he looked over the footlights and saw Emile's face level with his and all Johnny could say was: "Do you speak Spanish?"

One of my lifelong friends has been a dancer, who was the feminine half of an adagio act known as Holt and Gillis. Sheila Holt was a ballerina superb and she was booked to play fairy in pantomime at Hanley in the Potteries.

She was like a fairy, small, beautifully shaped and her every movement sheer poetry. Her job was to open the pantomime with a short little monologue. You know the sort of thing:

> Good children all, and grown ups too,
> Yet once again we bring to you
> The joys of pantomime ...

We had to do a first performance to a theatre full of kids from the Michelin Tyre people.

Unfortunately, they had been allowed to come into the theatre over an hour before any curtain up and they were restless. They were each given, as part of the treat, an apple, an orange and some sweets. But by the time our fairy made her way through the curtain, looking like a dream and expecting the usual, "Ahh, here's the fairy", the mood was a little different to what she anticipated.

It came as something of a shock for her to hear from such

tiny mites: "Cor, look at those legs," and before she could utter a word she was bombarded with orange peel, apple cores and sweets.

It's the only time I have seen a fairy ducking missiles whilst telling of the joys of fairyland. Come to think of it, it's the first time I have ever heard a sweet looking fairy say of the children, "The sexy little bastards!"

There has always been something pathetic about the theatre. Many of our great funny men were infinitely sad inside.

Like Claude Lester. Claude was probably the best known alcoholic in the business. He used to be fined every time he went on drunk and often he had very little or no salary to come.

To give you some idea of this strange man's way of life, he was once going to a band call with his wife. She was a woman I had great sympathy and regard for, remembering what my own mother had to put up with, and Claude was ten times worse than my old man. Mrs Lester was half of the act as the "feed". He heaved the two great bags aboard the bus and shoved them under the stairs, together they made their way to a seat and almost immediately he said something which must have annoyed her because she slapped his face.

With Shakespearean aplomb he raised himself up and shouted at the top of his voice: "Stop the bus."

"Sit down Claude, you're making a fool . . ."

"Woman, 'tis I, Claude Lester. You'll rue the day, stop the bus! Stop the bus, I say!"

The bus stopped, Mrs. Lester doing her best to make him be reasonable and quieten down. But he would have none of it and as he made his complaining way to the platform, she followed him.

He paused a moment, pulled the bags out from under the stairs, lifted them on to the pavement, then took his wife by the arm and assisted her off the bus. She stood by the pavement bewildered, and Claude stepped smartly back on to the bus and leaving his wife standing there with all the theatrical gear, he commanded in a loud voice to the conductor: "Drive on!"

A lifetime of this must have driven the poor woman round the bend.

He finished up in a bad way. They used to lock him in his room between houses so he couldn't get drunk before the second performance. However, at one theatre, after locking him in, he bribed the call boy with a note under the door to pop around the corner and get him a bottle of scotch.

A further bribe and the boy got him a straw and he had a bottle of scotch from a straw through the keyhole. When they opened up he was on his back and foaming at the mouth.

The pity of it all was, that Claude was a brilliant comedian, as most pros who knew him will agree.

A particularly pathetic example also comes to mind of the adverts in the stage for work, especially at the outbreak of war. Naturally no one wanted to sign you up for a contract you couldn't fulfil, and if your call-up papers were due then you were not to be considered. I remember one advert which read:

WANTED. DEMON KING. MUST BE MEDICALLY UNFIT.

*

I had been augmenting my meagre earnings on the stage by song writing, which brought in a few tenners and fivers.

To be a song writer of any standing one had practically to "live" in Tin Pan Alley. It has always been possible for someone from the outside to wallop in with a natural, like the two sisters who wrote *Cruising down the River*, but in the main, you had to be on the job to know who was publishing what, in the song world.

The song writers themselves, like Jimmy Kennedy,

Michael Carr, Leo Towers, Harry Leon, Tommie Connor, and other great tunesmiths, had a code of ethics. If one of them had written a cowboy song that had a chance, none of the others would submit a cowboy song until it was published, and the same with "tear" songs, which were referred to as "onions". They worked this so well that they were able to sell a song to the opposition instead of spoiling the chances of the others.

I remember little Tommie Connor, one of the best lyric writers in the game, sitting in the cafe at the top end of Charing Cross Road. With him were Reg Morgan, myself, and Percy Hirons of Feldmans. Tommie signalled for Kay, the Irish head waitress, to join us. He pulled out a crumpled piece of paper and began to sing. I think Tommie would be the first to agree that his singing was nothing to rave about, but a quietness descended as he sang it.

He's the little boy that Santa Claus forgot.

Before he had finished the chorus Kay was in tears with the sadness of it all, and the men had lumps in their throats. We KNEW he was on a winner. Within a few days it was printed and being sung everywhere.

Tommie followed that with *I'm Writing a Letter to Santa Claus* which Gracie Fields sang to the troops overseas.

Another smash hit.

Then, some years later, he crowned them both with *I Saw Mummy Kissing Santa Claus.*

Only a little man, but what a great song writer.

Michael (*South of the Border*) Carr, was a particular friend of mine and if we never saw each other for years on end, I could always expect a phone call from him on Christmas Day, from wherever he was in the world.

Tolchard Evans and Stanley Damerell were also great friends to me as a youngster in the business, and although they turned out many hits, I think perhaps my favourite of theirs is *Lady of Spain.*

As a song writer you were liable to meet everyone in

32

Tin Pan Alley and one of the regular visitors was a nice little girl in a red coat and long blonde hair. She became my neighbour for many years in Finchley and to this day she hasn't changed very much; in fact for the better part of her life she has been "the girl next door" to the nation. Her name: Vera Lynn.

You would see all the band leaders, the organists, singers like Richard Tauber, and musicians like Rachmaninoff, Charlie Ancliffe and Monte (*Butterflies in the Rain*) Ewing.

It was a world within a world, and just about the most perfect place to get the rough edges knocked off you in preparation for show business.

*

The war drums began to roll and things began to change. New titles were soon to be heard being sung round the world.

Michael Carr came up with *We're Gonna Hang Out the Washing on the Siegfried Line*. Hughie Charles entered the arena with *There'll Always be an England*. I came up with *Forget Me Not Lane*.

Then they flooded in:
I'll be Seeing You
We'll Meet Again
White Cliffs of Dover

At the time when Britain thought that the Maginot Line was a safe barrier and the BEF was settled in, I was serving with ENSA and teamed up with Joe Loss and his band. It was a good combination, for apart from Joe and his band, who were tops with the "boys" the show included The Carlisle Cousins, Chick Henderson, Monte Rey, Jack and Eddie Eden and me.

We started at a place called Lille, and did about four thousand two hundred miles of one-night stands. Every show was a riot. I was told that I could be as blue as I liked for it was, at that time, all men, and who was to know whether it was to be their last show ever.

I seem to have been a natural for the Forces as an entertainer. I think it was because at that time I was "one of the boys", the "other ranks" as they were referred to, and yet I was in a position to playfully poke fun at any pomposity of the higher ups. I could always find something to say that would hit the nail on the head.

I would walk on and pick on a sergeant, and say something like: "Look at the sergeant down there, smiling as if he's in his right mind! Sergeants, they're all the same, like bloody racehorses . . . once the tapes go up there's no holding them!"

Then, of course, there were the officers. When I referred to an officer as "A lemon with too many pips", I was home and dry.

The higher up the scale, of course, the bigger the laugh and so one just had to knock the CO.

"Here fellas, I tell you one thing, I've found out that at least you get the same food as the officers – only they get it first! We had to wait a hell of a time for the grub in the officers mess. Chicken! I asked the orderly what was taking so long. He said: 'It's the CO he wants *stuffing*!' "

With the band behind me listening to my performances every night, they naturally got used to the material and after hearing it a couple of times, the danger for me was that they would sit there behind me with stony faces. I therefore had to vary my act at each performance, so as to keep them laughing as well. It called for a great deal of new material.

At one particular show we were honoured by a visit of some VIPs headed by the Duke of Gloucester. He sent for Joe Loss and myself after the show.

Joe looked at me and said: "I think you've blotted your copybook this time, Chas, if he didn't like your gags it's the Tower!"

We went like a pair of schoolboys to the headmaster.

Standing at the top end of a long table full of VIPs I said: "Good evening sir, you sent for us!"

The Duke looked up and replied. "Ah yes, I just wanted to tell you how much I enjoyed the show," he told us, and then said to me, "You certainly know a lot of stories."

"Yes sir," I answered. "And a I know a lot more."

"I thought you might, and I dare you to sit there and tell me *every* story you know!" he said.

"Well, sir, I *dare* you to sit there and listen," I replied, pulling up a chair.

He did, for over three hours!

On that occasion I was reminded of an earlier show in Tallavera Barracks in Aldershot when I told a gag about a guardsman outside Buckingham Palace. He was marching up and down when a little man tapped him on the shoulder and said: "Excuse me, do you know me?"

The guardsman halted and whispered out of the corner of his mouth: "Bugger off, I'm busy!"

The little man undaunted, however, kept at him.

"Well look at me, surely you know me!"

He got the same response, only with more venom. "Bugger off. I've told you, I'm on duty. I'm on guard here!"

"But you *must* know me!" he insisted.

The guardsman had had enough. "Look, I don't know you and I don't bloody well want to know you."

"Well I'm the Duke of Connaught!"

The guardsman smartly presented arms and as he did so he punctuated each movement with a 'Jesus Christ almighty'!

In the mess afterwards, the very young officer sitting next to me said "I *did* enjoy your joke about the Duke of Connaught. He's my uncle you know."

True life happenings are always funnier than concocted stories, and it was in Lyons, where the show converged, that an amusing episode took place.

Gracie Fields was travelling from west to east with one show. Will Fyffe and a party was going in another direction, and we were going more or less in a zig zag lines from east to west.

We all met up at Lyons.

Will Fyffe was standing in the bar at the hotel where a number of us were billetted and he was trying to make some old Brigadier laugh. Will, however, was fighting a losing battle, for the old boy just leaned on the counter of the bar on one elbow, covering half his face with his hand and looked through Will with a stony stare.

After doing his best to get a laugh from the old boy for what seemed an age, someone from the doorway yelled ... "Will, for Christ's sake come to bed, he's fast asleep, he's got a glass eye."

The snow was so thick when we arrived in Lille, the trombone players had to warm their instruments over oil stoves before they could get the slides working.

We all went down at some time or other with 'flu, and at one time, I was sat wrapped in blankets at the side of the stage. I stumbled on to do my bits and leaned on the mike for support, then went back to sitting with a blanket around me.

I was taken very ill on the train and someone had arranged for an ambulance to take me to hospital on arrival. Instead I was carried secretly on a stretcher round the back of the train and looked after by the boys, because they were afraid that I might be kept in and they would lose track of me.

It was quite customary for a large crowd of us to go out together, and one morning, freezing with cold, we went into a place that had a bar and discovered that they also served hot coffee.

While we all stood around drinking it, however, a bell suddenly rang, and before we knew it, a door of a stairway opened and the place was suddenly alive with girls in all stages of undress. It was a brothel, and although most of us escaped fairly quickly, it was not before I had heard some remarks that were funnier than some of my gags.

We managed to get out before Dunkirk.

The funniest joke of all to me though, was during the evacuation of Dunkirk. I received a letter from ENSA asking if I would like to go back there.

My brother George, who had been on reserve had naturally been recalled and was one of the lads who underwent some of the worst experiences of the beaches.

As things hung in limbo I worked one or two places, but the blackout had almost killed the variety halls. I did play the County Theatre, Bedford and shared top of the bill with Robin Richmond the swing organist.

On the bill with us was an act known as Professor Sparks and Thelmina, the Electric Lady. This was a comedy act where the mad professor had an enormous machine like a tower on the stage, which generated electricity. Professor Sparks would hold two swords and touch the great tower with one and then touch his wife with the other, while she stood holding a six inch nail by a pair of tongs in each hand – over a bucket. The audience would then see the nail get white hot with the current passing through her body and finally she snapped the nail. It was very impressive. The secret of the machine was that the small voltage appeared to come from the top of the machine, and the lower he touched it, the greater the current.

The highlight of the act was a feature called, washing the electric baby, which involved audience participation. The more the participants dipped the dish mop in the water to wash the metallic baby the more the electricity would be amplified until they could hardly move – their grotesque endeavours were very funny. The Professor himself was not the most likeable of men and to loudly expound his beliefs and theories of the Blackshirts at such a time was foolish in the extreme. Robin Richmond was not slow to show how much he disagreed with him. Just before a show one night, Robin told the Professor to button his lip and stop shooting his mouth off about Blackshirts and there was a terrific argument and Robin, small as he was compared to Sparks, chinned the big man.

The Professor went on stage furious and, with all the spite in him, gave his wife and son all the electric shocks they could take, with Robin standing in the wings calling him all the terrible names he could lay his tongue to.

Poor Robin, he went on later, and while he was playing his electric organ, the Professor got his own back by kicking out the leads carrying the current and there was the shared top of the bill swinging away and getting nothing but silence.

Just before I received my call-up papers I was engaged to do a show, a late night cabaret for Carl Hyson, at the Grosvenor House Hotel in Park Lane.

My career was at last beginning to blossom. It was a huge show all about racing; staged because the war had stopped Ascot week. The show, naturally, was called *Ascot*. In it I had to play the part of a comic, a racing tipster, as well as do a long sketch as Ras Prince Monolulu, the most famous of all tipsters, complete with full feathered head-dress and robe.

Finally I had to compere the great hobby-horse race in which film stars and anyone of note were invited to take part in a race on hobby horses, which were a new rage at that time.

Carl Hyson was a marvellous producer, and his girls, The Carl Hyson Girls, were a sort of legend. They were each given, or loaned – I'm not sure which – a fur coat and were allowed a hairdo each week, and if any one of them walked in looking anything less than a film star or millionairess, she was sacked on the spot. They would even get the push for wearing a headscarf.

Sad to say it was short lived for me. My call-up papers arrived and I was informed that I was to report for duty with, of all regiments, The Irish Fusiliers.

CHARLIE CHESTER

*The world will have advanced
when the gaining of knowledge
means more than the knowledge
of gaining.*

CHAPTER THREE

What a pity that the power of
thought and reason
gives some people the reason for
thoughts of power.

IF ever I thought I was a funny man, I certainly had to look
to my laurels in the Army, for therein lies some of the
greatest wits in the world.

Conscripted almost to a man, none of us wanted to be
there anyway and I wondered if, after all my struggles to
get somewhere in showbiz, this was to be the end of it all.

The breakthrough was within my grasp, I could feel it,
and with a number of broadcasts to my credit I had become
a popular name, although not by any standards, "famous".

Now I was one of the many, lost in a welter of khaki.

My name was sufficiently big enough to have the fact
announced that Cheerful Charlie Chester had "joined" an

Irish regiment and that Al Bollington had gone into the Air Force, with both of us pictured in the *Daily Mirror*.

The train was full of cockneys making their way to Newtown in Wales. Sad, dejected, apprehensive, talkative. Sitting next to me was a real rough diamond, a man who later became a great friend. MacQuillan had no fear. He was rough, tough, stocky, wearing corduroys and, when he spoke he punctuated every other word with "effin' ".

I didn't know it at the time, but by virtue of his Army number this was the man who would fall in, always alongside of me.

He was reading the *Daily Mirror* when suddenly he took a hard look at me and saw that it was my picture in the paper.

"Ere . . . you ain't 'im are you? Cheerful effin' Charlie! Gawd stone me."

His approval of me was evident. He liked me. Before long the whole train knew that some sort of celebrity was among them. Being a professional comedian they looked to me for some laughs and I felt less inclined at that time than they could possibly know.

I was dressed in my best stage suit, made at Ostlings of Albemarle Street, when Peter Brough (who became the renowned ventriloquist with his dummy Archie) was the man who measured me. I looked a dandy with my grey trilby hat and my guitar on the rack in its black shaped case.

"I'm from Wormwood effin' Scrubs," MacQuillan informed me. "They told me I could ever join the effin' Army, or finish me effin' sentence, so I decided to join the effin' Army." The fluidity with which he could insert the effs was amazing.

As I said before though, he had no fear. Where some of the lads would jump to it and almost die of fright when the sergeant major or an officers spoke to them, Mac simply brushed authority to one side.

On arrival at Newtown we were a newly formed regiment, the 6th Battalion and part of the Irish Brigade, comprised of the Inniskillins, the Irish Fusiliers and the Irish Rifles.

We were taken to what looked like an enormous hanger on the outskirts of the little town. It wasn't an aeroplane hanger, I never knew what it really was, but there were tiers and tiers of seats facing an arena and the palliasses were laid along these tiers. The only trouble was, if you turned over sharply, you were liable to fall right through. When lights out came and all was dark as pitch, one man Bob Meginnis was weeping (I discovered he'd just got married) and others were giggling wondering what the hell was going to happen next. Then the Sergeant Major (Kelly) who had rather red rimmed eyes, came in and shouted: "No talking."

From Mac's direction came the reply in the darkness. "Rubbish!"

There was a stunned silence for a moment, then: "Who said that?"

From the darkness again. "Me. Shove off."

During the laughter that followed, there was a scuffle as the irate Sergeant Major climbed his way over the bodies, stepping on them and over them in an endeavour to discover the cuplrit.

Being MacQuillan, he was situated near me, of course.

Finally he found MacQuillan and as he grabbed him by the rough shirt he was sleeping in, hissed: "Listen sonny, you'll have plenty of time to be funny later. You're in the Army now, and you'll learn to do as you're told.'

Mac, in a hurt voice said, "Oh please. You're crumpling my pyjamas."

Kelly let go and went on. "It's your first night in the Army, so I'll let it go for now, but in the ordinary way you'd be inside the bloody guardhouse. So just pipe down."

Mac had spent his life rejecting authority, or at least hating it, and with a snarl he retorted. "You listen to me bleedin' red-eyed Kelly. You don't scare me, I don't give a hoot for any of you, so move off."

It wasn't the best way to start an Army career.

Kelly gave him a hell during our training and when we were told that we were shortly to go into action, we were asked if we had any questions.

MacQuillan stood up.

"Have you got a question, MacQuillan?"

"No, Sergeant Major. Just some effin' good advice, when we *do* go into action, whatever you do, don't stand anywhere in front of my rifle."

I shuddered.

On arrival, however, our first job was to be kitted out and then medically inspected.

Being a newly formed regiment they had little of anything in the way of modern equipment.

The bantering was incessant and I discovered that the Regiment was comprised of Irish officers and non-commissioned officers and one or two Irish lads, but the main body of the men were equally divided between London Cockneys and lads from the Potteries.

We were still in our civilian clothes and after breakfast, such as it was, with kippers and jam ladled into the same mess tin, we were lined up in front of the Regimental Sergeant Major. He had a real Cockney accent and in full voice, in front of the timid Welsh onlookers (mostly ladies) he went on. "Now, maybe you don't want to be here, but that's not my concern, you all know that there's a war on, and you're in it right up to your necks. Now believe it or not, we're going to make soldiers of you, and you can either do it the hard way, or the easy way, it's entirely up to you. You'll learn how to fight, how to use a rifle and you'll be made up into companies and platoons. We need cooks and office staff and other specialised people and the rest of you will be trained as fighting men."

"While you are here, you will be expected to do guard duty on a rota system. Until you have learned to use a rifle, however, it will be in the form of 'stick duty' (this meant you walked around with a damn great pick axe handle instead of a rifle). It works out that from the nine hundred odd men here, so many will be in HQ, then there's transport, officers' batmen, company cooks, stores and so on, and for the remainder it means one night in five stick duty.

After the opening lecture we were told to undress and turn our pants back to front so that the fly hole was at the rear. This was because they had no shorts for us.

We were then lined up in sections and made to jog trot through the town, wearing nothing but reversed pants, to the stores, where we were kitted out with boots, khaki uniform, denims and all the accoutrements, knife, fork, spoon and so on.

When I put mine on, the neck line was so enormous you could almost see my navel. I had to have it tailored and then discovered that I was allergic to khaki, so I also had to have a velvet insert in the collar band to prevent getting a rash.

Although it carried no promotion, I was almost immediately made a platoon commander, which is only a glorified phrase for prefect.

The lads liked me and I used to serenade them with my guitar, and being a comic, I had plenty of material to give them a laugh.

I did make one mistake, however, it was at PT. We had to learn what they termed unarmed combat, and a particularly sprightly corporal was detailed to teach us. And he *knew* he was good at his job.

I could never fight or box very well, but I had learned judo in the Sea Cadets. (I actually gave a display at Crystal Palace, dressed as the woman who has her handbag stolen, and to do this I had further tuition from a Japanese gentleman called Mr Matsuoka, who taught the police).

I now found myself years later being beckoned by the corporal saying: "You, you'll do. Now I'm coming at you, what are you going to do?" and with that he launched himself towards me.

My reflexes automatically took over and although I hadn't even thought about this sort of thing all those years, the corporal went sailing over my head. I knew I had done the wrong thing.

"I see," said the corporal getting up. "Clever fella eh?"

"Sorry corporal."

"You're *going* to be sorry." And for a while, I was.

I must be sensible. I must think. That's what I kept telling myself.

Some time later they had what they termed Interior Economy and we were all asked if we had any suggestions for improving our lot. This, I thought, was more up my street, the ideas man. There could be no harm in making good sensible suggestions.

"Yes sir."

"Good, what is it?" The officer beamed at me.

"Well, sir, with nine hundred men here, and all those nine hundred large drinking mugs stacked like that over there, with all the dust from the Welsh Hills blowing in and half filling them, wouldn't it be a better idea if they were stacked upside down, the dust wouldn't get into them?"

"Now, there you are. That *is* a good idea men, that's what we want, good ideas for improvement."

Then he pointed his little cane at me. "Now I'll tell you what you do, you go over there and wash every one of those mugs out, and re-stack them the other way up."

Why didn't I keep my big mouth shut?

I had friends in the newspaper business and they sent us some footballs and sports gear. We needed more. Lots more.

The Colonel sent for me. He was most interested that I should have obtained the stuff for the Regiment and was even more interested in me as a performer.

Was it possible to fix up some sort of entertainment?

"Well, sir, I have already made enquiries and there isn't one professional in the Regiment, but there are two possible piano players and Ronnie Moss in my company is good at monologues. It will mean that if I got something together, they would only be as strong as the material I gave them, and to train them into anything like a concert party I should need time, and time off to do it."

At last I was spared from route marching and potato harvest picking.

I formulated a programme of sketches. I had a good Irish tenor called Spud Murphy (who was later killed by a mortar bomb) who had a glorious voice, but at the slightest whim he would go off key and it was a hell of a job to get him back. This meant that the pianist had to be competent enough to change at the same time.

I was down for a couple of patter and song spots, and I had a group which I had formed into a choir. This was the basis of a show.

I had to teach them timing, how to get the best laughs out of the cross-over gags. It was a hell of a task. The lads, however, were so willing and they really put their soul into it. They followed my every word and a more loyal band of associates I have never known.

The manager of a small local cinema, The Regent, Newtown, was, strangely enough, named George Black, a Manxman. He approached me and asked if I would like to put the show on at his cinema instead of him running the Sunday film.

As soon as the posters went up the place was sold out in advance and the show put on by The Craziliers was a sensation. So much so, that we not only put on regular shows there, but we even had to take it to Welshpool and perform in that cinema too.

Being a concert party meant double work for us, because even though we got some time off to rehearse the major part of our time was spent soldiering. It was months later I said we would not go on with the shows unless we were relieved of guard duty.

My humble concert party made enough money for the

Regiment to buy a complete set of pipes and drums for the band and all the sports kit we needed.

For St Patrick's Day, we had to make special preparation, and four days before the event we had to start the polishing, marching and drilling for the ceremony of the Shamrock.

Oh God, what a performance, especially with MacQuillan at the side of me. Even the leather parts of our braces had to be polished, and believe it or not, the soles of our boots and our fly buttons.

Daily we went through the routine of the parade.

It all worked out on the eventful day like this.

Firstly we knew that by lunch time, every man in the Regiment would be offered a free pint of beer, and would have the afternoon off.

We were marched to the great parade ground in companies and platoons, accompanied by the band in orange kilts, bagpipes wailing.

The individual (Irish) sergeant would stand in front of his men and we were drilled for the reception of the full Colonel, visiting us specially for the occasion.

We would be given the order to secure arms, which meant placing the rifle in between your legs and gripping it with your knees. This left the hands free.

The left hand would remain close to the side and the order would come: "Three cheers for the Colonel of the Regiment." At this we were supposed to remove our forage caps from the head with the right hand, and as you shouted "hooray", it was lifted to the full extent of the right arm and then placed on the right shoulder, still holding it. This was repeated three times, and if you've ever tried to replace a forage cap with one hand, you'll know what an impossible task it is.

After so many rehearsals the men were heartily sick of all this nonsense, and by the time the actual cheer was supposed to be given there was a high wind and the officer in whose honour it was, must have learned the truth about how they felt, for almost to a man they said the same thing – quietly, it's true, but with so many doing the same thing it sounded so very loud.

"Three cheers for the Colonel of the Regiment! Hip Hip . . ."

"Eff him!"

Our Irish sergeant wasn't terribly happy about this and it began to show.

The next routine of this Regimental farce was for the officers to fall in a line. There was a roll of drums and the Irish pipes (which I had helped to provide) stopped wailing.

The officers in a line were presented to the Colonel by the Lieutenant-Colonel, all receiving a piece of Shamrock to place in their caps.

After this the warrant officers were presented. Then the sergeants went forward to receive theirs and after affixing the green plumage to their hats, they were each given a large tray filled with dirty little dollops of mud, one piece for each man in the ranks.

This was done as a drill movement and as the sergeant came nearer pace by pace, all very military. "Take a piece of shamrock" . . . another pace . . . "Take a piece of Shamrock." Then he reached MacQuillan standing on my right.

"Take a piece of Shamrock!"

"Eff it!"

There was a stunned silence. The sergeant didn't want anyone to know he was having trouble on such an important occasion.

Menacingly now. "Take a piece of Shamrock."

"Stick it up your arse. I ain't Irish!"

By now they were eyeball to eyeball and the sergeant spoke in the only language Mac seemed to know.

"Take a piece of effin' Shamrock!" Mac took a piece, looked at it with disdain and threw it at the feet of the sergeant. Before he know what had happened, two men fell out, arrested him and took him to the guardhouse. He deserved it, of course.

Many years later, after the war, I bumped into an old comrade who told me that Mac probably saved the life of the company tailor who was undertrained and not really ready for battle. Mac apparently apologized to him before knocking him out cold and laying him in a trench. He later reported that he thought Jock had been hit for he saw him fall. But no one knew the full story. It would seem that most of the gold in this world is hidden beneath the dirt, it just needs finding.

Some of the regular soldiers and NCOs of our Regiment were those reputed to have beaten the German Army at marathon marching, so you can well imagine how good they were at footslogging.

I do know that after we moved to Bangor in North Wales we were the fastest thing ever to cross the Menai Bridge. Traffic was restricted to four miles an hour so when we broke step and did a forced march over it, we were faster than the traffic.

The longest route march I ever did was thirty-seven-and-a-half miles in one day. I never want to attempt it again.

The worst one, however, was the march between Bangor and Holyhead, twenty-eight miles.

We were more than sorry to leave Newtown. The folks of that homely little Welsh town took to us completely and made us really welcome. My Regiment had adopted my song *Forget Me Not Lane* as a marching song and when we finally left the town the entire establishment of Price Jones factory, overlooking the station, leaned out of their windows and sang it as only the Welsh can. It brought many a tear to the eyes. Especially mine.

It was with the money I earned from this song that Reg Morgan and I started a music publishing company – the Victory Music Publishing Company.

Reg, an older man than myself, was not eligible for the Services and it was agreed that I should put an equal amount into the company and survive on my Army pay, while he would take salary and expenses and pay the secretary.

We discovered a young singer called Jimmy Groom and were so convinced he was a star in the making, we employed him to wrap parcels in the music company as he was medically unfit for service. I suggested a new name for him: Steve Conway.

He earned more wrapping parcels than I did as a sergeant but it wasn't long before he became the singing star we all expected, and sadly passed away at the peak of his young career.

I wrote a book called the *Kiddies Sing-Song Sketch Book* It was an idea where kiddies could learn to read verses, draw characters, and have little songs about them all in one.

I remember my excitement at receiving a telegram from Reg: FIRST ORDER SING SONG BOOK FROM W. H. SMITHS £3,541 WORTH. I was over the moon. I was skint, and yet that was just the first order.

Next I wrote a series of greetings cards, they were individual little verses, To my Mother, Sister, Brother, Friend, Wife, etc, and they all carried an original personal verse to fit the recipient. The idea also carried a small square in which a photograph could be inserted, and my thoughts behind this were that if the person sending it did not return, here was a permanent reminder in verse, with a picture of the loved one.

We had a colossal order from Woolworths and I began to think that although I was just another squaddie who was stony broke, there was something saved for after the war.

Reg and I repaid ourselves the £500 each we put in, but other than that, for me, it was a rather disappointing episode.

I remember asking Reg about managing me after the war, and he explained that the music company would take all his time and that he would hand me over to a man called Sidney Grace. Although in the Army himself, Sidney was demobbed before me, and as a theatrical agent, he was second to none.

It was while I was in Bangor, North Wales, that I was billeted with a family high on a mountainside. My wife was staying with me, which made life easier in many ways.

The town of Bangor itself lies in a great hollow and from the house one could look right across the town to the other side. I was standing knee deep in snow one chilly night and the German bombers were heard going overhead towards Liverpool. It was thirteen minutes past seven and all alone I looked into the blackness, when suddenly I saw some flashing lights, from the direction of Bangor College. They seemed to sending a sort of morse signal. I can't read or send morse, so I wrote the dots and dashes with a stub of pencil on the plain blue side of a match box.

I ran like the wind and contacted our Major Flewitt, who made me tap out the message repeatedly, and at the end of it all, he had written down a series of letters. N.W.U. N.W.U. N.W.U.

"North Wales University!" he shouted, and later at Bangor College two culprits were arrested.

I staged a pantomime in Bangor with my boys, together with a set of lovely girls from the Liverpool and Victoria Insurance Company.

We made a handsome profit for the Regiment and with those lovely ladies to work alongside, the boys agreed it was the best "duty" they'd ever done.

After marching to our new station at Tre Arddur Bay near Holyhead on the Isle of Anglesey, I was asked to broadcast a regimental show from the Convent at Holyhead. Although we had presented many shows, my boys had never done a broadcast, and they considered this was a great honour for them.

I had to prepare all the scripts and this took a good deal of time and hard work because now we had to be in the "professional" class. Besides, it had to be good for my own name's sake.

I had left my portable typewriter back in the digs at Bangor and because I'd been refused permission to use one in the office I decided to go against orders and make my own way by bus to Bangor.

When I returned, I was on a charge for being two hours outside the barrack area without permission.

I explained that I couldn't put on the show without having the use of my typewriter. The Captain tried to be understanding but standing orders had been broken. I got seven days CB.

Confined to barracks for doing them a favour!

I was up early in the morning on fatigue parade. Scrubbing floors and every evening peeling the eternal spuds. Reporting every hour, full battledress one time, and denims the next. I began to feel that running the concert party wasn't worth it.

I was scrubbing the floor of the great mess hall one day, and I saw two pairs of polished shoes at my side. Looking up I saw the smiling faces of RSM Larkin and the Padre. They seemed to think it was terribly funny.

"How are you getting on then Charlie?"

"Oh fine thank you ... sir," I added with deliberation. "I've come to the conclusion that I'll be a soldier and forget the concert party; it's not worth it."

Their smiles vanished. "Don't be like that, it's all in the game you know."

"It's a game I'm not enjoying very much. There are a few people who think that organising a show is easy. If this is the thank you, I don't want to know ... sir."

Somehow my colour sergeant found another reason for having me on a further charge and I got another seven days.

This made up my mind for me.

Again I had a visit whilst scrubbing from the RSM and the Padre.

"Charlie, you're always scrubbing, you're like the Irish

53

Washerwoman." The Padre thought it was an extremely funny joke.

"Yes sir, I am, I've washed my hands of the so-called concert party, that's for sure."

"Aw come on now, don't be silly, you can't do that!"

"Can't I? Oh no sir, I've had enough, I've done nothing but try to improve the status of the Regiment with all the work I've put in, and there are too many ready to knock me for it. Give it to somebody else . . . sir!"

"Stop scrubbing! And that's an order!"

I stopped.

"Now, look here Charlie. What's a few days CB? It's nothing really, and after all you haven't got much to do now have you? Besides, we want to talk to you about the special show!"

"There is no special show as far as I'm concerned," I said.

"Oh yes there is. It's a special show to honour the return of Lieutenant-Colonel Russell."

"Well sir, much as I think the Colonel is a grand chap, I'm afraid I won't be doing one. My mind is made up."

There was a pregnant silence for a moment and RSM Larkin quietly said, "If I remember rightly, you are due for a leave soon aren't you?"

"Yes, sir."

"Well let me put it this way . . . No show . . . No leave."

I was cornered. I imagined that he could stop my leave and I'd do anything rather than lose that.

I agreed to do the show, but I was furious at the way it was done and I had my own thoughts on its production.

I decided that the best way to do it was to make it a crazy variety show which I would compere. As I had been "order-ed" to do it against my will, I did it as a command.

I marched on in military style. Halted. Turned left. Stood at ease. Then, standing easy. "Sir. Complying with orders issued on such and such a date, I herewith present to you one show."

Each entrance I rubbed their noses in it the only way I knew.

At the interval, Colonel Russell, who was still and ever mindful of the good that the concert party had done, asked me what was wrong.

When he discovered that I was ordered to do the performance on a no-show-no-leave basis, he was furious too.

What he said to the RSM and the Padre was nobody's business. Shortly afterwards I was promoted to Corporal.

On that occasion, I realized that grudges are not always nursed, for as I was told of my promotion, the RSM shouted the usual: "Left turn, quick march," and as we stood outside the CO's room the RSM said to me: "And if you're not properly dressed inside five minutes, you're on another charge."

"Me," I said. "Not properly dressed?"

"Yes, you haven't got those bloody stripes stitched on yet . . . Corporal!" Then he smiled and winked.

After that there took an unusual turn of events for me. There were plenty of fifth columnists around and security had to be tightened everywhere.

Colonel Russell sent for me and I could sense by the atmosphere that something different was afoot.

"I've sent for you because you are an actor," he said. "Now I have a job for you that I think is right up your your street. You don't *have* to do it, and it could be dangerous in a way, but being used to disguises you could help the war effort. It's to do with field security and counter espionage. Now do you want to volunteer?"

"Yes sir."

"Right. Now, firstly my officers and NCOs will be informed that you are to be left entirely alone, you will come and go as you like under the instructions of this man." He handed me a piece of paper with a major's name on it and a map reference. Just a single number.

"You will report there first thing tomorrow morning and good luck."

"Yes sir, and thank you sir."

When I arrived at the map reference it was a disused garage out in the wilds of nowhere.

The Major lectured a group of us on field security and counter espionage for about an hour and told us that we had been chosen as candidates who would have to prove our astuteness, for we were to be "dummy" fifth columnists.

We would be given specific tasks to perform and in doing them we must wreak as much havoc and damage as possible (on paper). "You won't actually cut the telephone wires for instance, but you make a note of where and how you could have, leaving proof of the fact!"

My first assignment was to "Break unauthorised into a place known as Soldier's Rock at Tenby, and furnish evidence that you have unalwfully visited the gun pits. They have two eight inch coastal battery guns there."

I was told that I could go in a guise of my own choosing, but that there would be at least one mistake on my papers so that there was a possibility and a probability of my being caught.

After a good deal of thought, I asked if I could have an accomplice as I wished to go as an armourer sergeant from Carmarthen Headquarters. The Major agreed and I took a stocky little man called Wally Baker.

Equipped with the necessary cap badges and armed with a reaming rod (a specialised tool used by Armourers) together with papers that contained obvious mistakes, the pseudo "Private" Wally Baker and I made our way to Soldiers' Rock.

I told Wally to let me do all the talking while he should appear to be a bit dumb, which he did. I also arranged that if we were challenged and things got sticky, I would bend down to do up my bootlaces, which would be a cue to start punching and then run.

The long lane that led to the camp was straight and cut across open country. My story would be that the truck had packed up some distance away and rather than waste time we had decided to walk it while the repairs were on the way.

There was a large gate, not unlike a level crossing and close by was a Nissen hut. This was the guard room.

When I explained my business the security officer was sent for, a cultured and very dapper little man, who sat down to inspect our papers.

"What do you actually want then Sergeant?"

"Well sir, this is part of my round, it all comes under Carmarthen Headquarters, and I have orders to inspect the small arms for defaults."

"Well, actually, we do have one or two broken rifle butts," he said.

I nodded. "That's usual sir. No real problems though?"

"Not that I know of." At this point he began to go through the A.B.64s and the papers of authorisation starting from the top and I knew that sooner or later he couldn't fail to notice something wrong, if he did it line by line. My eyes had been listed as brown, and they were blue.

I looked out of the guard room window and quietly said, "Oh excuse me sir, I couldn't help noticing the allotments out there!"

He looked out of the window with me and I noticed a certain amount of pride. "Yes."

"Are they actually done by the men here?"

"Yes they are, why?"

"Well sir, I can only say that I've travelled around a good deal in this job and I haven't seen any better anywhere."

"Oh really, yes, well we grow our own potatoes, green stuff . . ."

He was warming to the subject, which at least kept him off our papers. Finally he grabbed my wrist and I thought the handcuffs were going on. My heart sank.

Instead, he picked up an indelible stamp, pushed my sleeve back and after dipping it on the pad, slapped it on my wrist, leaving a beautiful stamp there. Next he repeated the movement with Wally saying: "There, that's your pass in. Just show that to anyone and they'll know it's all right."

"Thank you sir. Oh, you won't mind if we use the NAAFI?"

"No, carry on Sergeant!"

I saluted him and Wally and I made our way through the gate which a sentry opened for us.

I not only visited the gun pits, I was in there for fifty-five minutes and had all their small arms laid out for inspection.

Somehow Wally and I made our way to the two great coastal battery guns and there I left my calling card. These were printed for me by Carl Hyson as "Bookies" cards which I used in the Ascot floor show at Grosvenor House (Cheerful Charlie gives you a run for your money). I left one up the breech of each gun and some in amongst the great shells standing on the platform.

We were nearly caught doing this. A squaddie asked us what we were doing and I quickly talked him into believing that we were looking for the NAAFI and couldn't resist the opportunity of having a quick look at the big guns. We got away with that too. But just as we were entering the NAAFI, bells began to ring and I realised I had overplayed it by leaving cards everywhere. Someone had obviously found one too soon.

"Easy does it Wally. Make your way slowly to the gate and we'll get out of here," I whispered.

"'Ere mate, you seen any strange bods knockin' about?"

"No mate, sorry."

"Oh never mind." He was off in a flash and men were dashing about everywhere, the bells ringing incessantly.

Wally and I sauntered towards the gate and went through it, but just as we were about fifty yards clear of it, we heard:

"Stop those two men . . . Oi you! Come back here."

It was a major, standing just outside the gate by the sentry.

"Don't forget Wally," I said quietly as we slowly walked back. "If I do my bootlace up, start swinging and run."

As we neared the major I heard him say, "Who are you?
What's your business?"

"Armourer sir, Carmarthen Headquarters. I've been
attending to all those broken butts."

The sentry stood by his box at the side of the gate. Wally
was nearest to him and the major confronted me.

"Have you been interrogated?"

"Yes sir," I said, showing the mark on my wrist.

"What did you say your name was?"

I told him and tried to sound casual.

"Where did you say you were from?"

"Carmarthen Headquarters sir."

"I see, what's the phone number there?"

He had me, that was the one thing I didn't know. I tried
to bluff my way out of it. I scratched my head and replied.
"You've got me there sir, I haven't had any occasion to use
it."

He paused for a moment. "I think you'd better come
back inside."

This was the end of the line. I knew that if I went back in
I was caught. I bent down to do my bootlace up and shouted:
"OK Wally" and with an almighty heave, he pushed the
major over the gate. I immediately ran back up the long
road and imagined that Wally was hot on my heels.

I had overlooked the sentry. After recovering from the
shock of what had just transpired, he grabbed Wally and
the major had now picked himself up off the floor.

"Stop that man!" I heard the command and kept running.

Then I heard the click of a rifle, and fortunately for me the
sentry was a new boy and didn't have one "up the spout".
I dread to think what might have happened if he had.

"Stop him!" I heard the call again and straight in front
of me walking towards me were two big soldiers. They
pounced and not only caught me but gave me a pretty rough
handling. Wally and I were in the guard house in a flash.

We had to sweat it out for a long time and finally the

little officer who first stamped our wrist, the one so proud of the men's gardening, came in to interrogate me. I explained that I was on field security and he just couldn't believe it.

"What do you claim to have done then?" he asked with a long face.

"Well sir, I not only unlawfully visited the gun pits, and had all your small arms laid out for inspection, I have blown up both your big guns – on paper, of course."

He went as white as a sheet. Someone would obviously be getting a hell of a rocket. "Well at least we caught you didn't we?" he said with some consolation.

"Yes sir, but I'm afraid you didn't really hold us," I said.

"What the hell do you mean?"

"Well sir, it's true that you grabbed us and put us here, but if you look in my haversack there, you'll find some little rolled balls of paper, they represent hand grenades. You never searched us before you put us here, and we could have blown our way out easily!" The poor man snatched my haversack and the rolled up paper balls fell out.

"Oh my God," he said, as if the world had come to an end.

"I'm sorry sir," I said, knowing that he would be for it.

He looked at me with almost tears in his eyes, and said . . . "Oh well, I'll tell you one thing Sergeant" – and with all the viciousness he could muster he hissed – "You must be just about the best fucking liar in the British Army!"

My next assignment was to steal papers from the officer in command, or at least papers from the desk of the second in command of an airfield. I was told that the RAF in question had been warned that their security would be tested within the month.

For this job I opted to go as a civilian. The thing I knew more about than any other was show business, and I decided to go as a representative of Drury Lane's ENSA.

A small brief case and just me, that's all that was needed. I got to the main guardroom and asked if I could see the entertainments officer and when he arrived I never even suggested that I wanted to go inside the place at all. I made it seem that I was quite content to talk my business right there in the guardroom.

Using a vivid imagination, and blinding the man with science, I explained. "I am a site assessor for the various types of shows for the services. They range, of course, from the four-handed gun site units, to the much larger fifteen-handed shows. These, of course, included the chorus girls, usually eight to a show, and naturally these could only be routed to places where they have the necessary facilities, stage size, toilets, dressing rooms and so on."

Oh yes, he quite saw that. They would like one of the larger shows with the girls though.

Naturally, and it would be possible to route them on that circuit provided all the facilities were there, for instance, did they have Stelmers? How many bays and batons were there? Were there any acting areas?

Although I'm sure that the poor soul had no idea what I was talking about, he tried to look as if he understood.

"Look old boy, why don't you come through and weigh the place up for yourself, you could see just what we have got."

"Well, if you're sure I'm not taking up your valuable time old chap!"

"Come on then, this way."

It was as easy as that.

Once in, it was a pretence at measuring up the stage, checking the accommodation for the "girls" to dress and when I explained that it would take some time to finish my calculations, he left me alone, saying that he would be back in half an hour.

Within that half hour I had done my job and nicked the papers from the top man's desk and was back on the stage waiting for the officer.

I'm sorry that he never got the fifteen-handed show he expected, with all the girls he was looking forward to entertaining in the mess. I know that I got a strange look from my Major, wondering how the hell I did it.

I have a feeling that my own Major sold me up the river after that. I was sent on another job to an outlying unit to steal something and wreak as much havoc as I could before leaving. I had a premonition on nearing the coastal site that all was not well, and instead of entering the front gate, as I originally intended, I detoured and went right round to the sea front and approached it by climbing up the cliff face.

This took me a long time, and when I edged as near to the main entrance as I dared I saw the machine gunners waiting to receive me. They had been phoned to warn them I was coming!

I laid there and drew a picture of my reception committee, then drew another picture of the lay-out of the camp and finally made my way back, and as I did so, I cut their telephone wires.

It was while I was engaged on this work that I was suddenly sent for by my Colonel. "I could stop you if I so desired," he told me, "but they want you to go to War Office and form a new regiment under Captain George Black, a regiment of professional entertainers. Would you like to go?"

"Yes sir, I would. I am naturally fond of the Regiment, but I feel this is something I would be very good at."

"I'm sure you would. Promise me that you will always wear the badge of the Irish Fusiliers and that you will continue to whiten your stripes and always look like an Irish Fusilier."

"Yes, sir, I promise!"

"Right. You leave on Friday morning. I don't like to let you go, but good luck – and Sergeant . . . your platoon can have the morning off to see you off at the station."

"Thank you sir."

A big salute and that was that. Well nearly!

The Sergeant Major gave me a farewell present: he made

me guard commander the night before I left. This meant
being on guard all night, and changing them every two
hours. The guard commander's room was in a large building that had a dance hall and this particular evening there
was a Regimental Dance.

Lieutenant-Colonel Russell attended and saw me marching out to change the guard.

He was furious that I should have been made to do that
on my last night and told the Sergant Major to bring me to
the bar.

At the time I was a non drinker but the Colonel insisted
that the injustice must be put right and I was ordered to
have a drink with him.

I did – a whisky and hated it. Then another, and another,
and before long I only just remember being carried to the
guard commander's room, and vaguely recall hearing the
Colonel say: ". . . and don't disturb him till the morning."

When I arrived at the RASC Depot at Greenford, I was,
as I had promised the Colonel, every inch an Irish Fusilier.
Shining cap badge, knife-edge crease in the trousers, boots
shone like black diamonds, and my thin white piped melton-
ian creamed stripes had been appended in the usual manner
with just one small section of hairs left on a cut away tooth
brush. As I walked smartly across the parade ground I
overheard one from the ranks say: "Cor Blimey. . . . Look at
that bleedin' Sergeant with the neon lighting!"

The formation of the regiment known as The Central
Pool of Artistes, or Stars in Battledress, as they were
known, had begun. Soldiers with *names* began arriving
from all over the country. Nat Gonella, Norman Wisdom,
Terry Thomas, Eugene Pini the violinist, Willy Solomons
the celebrated pianist. Bif Byfield, Sid Millward, Harry
Segal. Straight actors, musicians, comics, singers.

Later we had officers to produce the shows – men such
as Michael Dennison, James Hayter and Jack Carlton, but
they came much later and the first shows were produced by
George Black himself. Colonel Basil Brown was his im-

mediate superior, a man I have known and admired from those days to the present.

It was whilst writing the material for the shows that I began to spot one or two good performers who, up until then, had not made a name.

Corporal Ken Morris, late of Stephani's Silver Songsters, was a fine eccentric performer, and great pianist, and above all a good singer. Ken, brilliant though he was, could not read music. This was unfortunate, for I learned from Captain Black, that anyone who couldn't read music as a pianist, was no use and must be returned to their unit. We taught Ken in the lunch hour how the tunes went, and he memorized the copies so that when he had to play the various pieces for George Black it looked as if he were reading them. Ken was made pianist for the first of the shows to go out, and he was a sensation.

Although I was writing material for all the forthcoming shows, I had to take out the next.

We toured all the dumps and dives and Godforsaken places you can think of, leaving behind us a trail of laughter.

It was hard going being soldiers and professional entertainers at the same time. Our shows, especially at some of the outlying places were welcomed and looked forward to and, in the main, we were treated extremely well. But of course we did run into the "dyed in the wool" soldier types who thought we were just playing at soldiers, and after doing late shows, still expected us to rise with the bugle at 6 am. If we didn't they thought we were being "pampered".

There were times too, when the show was deeply appreciated and we were absolutely great, until we expected a hot meal, then we were considered a nuisance.

In all honesty though I can say that the Stars in Battledress companies did a fine job in keeping up the morale of the troops in almost every theatre of war. We weren't just little amateur groups putting on a party piece, we were staging professionally produced shows. We were hand-picked members with varying talents, with specially written material, carrying all our own props, piano, back flats, which we cleated together, microphones and speakers, and with all the official Army kit as well, we had plenty to do to keep loading up and unloading.

We were sent to all the various "commands" and we did a full two hour show, regardless of whether it was a garrison, or a gun site.

Once my party was routed to a "labour" force of the Pioneer Corps, which turned out to be the men who were too tough for Army prison. I remember it well because we had to post one of the company, the one who didn't happen to be on stage, outside our own billet in case our stuff was pinched while we did the show.

Being a "labour" prison camp, we had to share the same amenities as the men. Consequently our beds consisted of double tier bunks with a wire base and just a bale of straw for a mattress. Peter Kavanagh was stamping up and down one morning with straw in his mouth kicking backwards at the walls. When the Sergeant Major came in and asked him if he'd gone bloody mad, he replied: "No, we've got to live like bloody horses, I thought I'd act like one."

On another occasion, the show we gave went like a bomb . . . well, at least the music, singing and knockabout sketches did, and yet me, the principal comic, I died on my feet each time I went on. I couldn't understand it. I knew from all the other places that my material was good, but this worried me.

After the show I buttoned the entertainments officer and said. "What's the matter with your lot, didn't they like me or something?"

"Oh, yes," he said. "They loved the show, but they just didn't understand your bits. You see this is the Polish Brigade!"

This also happened again with the Spanish Brigade.

At one particular underground ammunition dump, I remember we had to perform on one platform, while the troops sat on another, for they used miniature trains to transport the ammunition underground. I can tell you that there's nothing so disconcerting as to start telling jokes and have to wait till the train goes by to finish them.

There came a time when someone asked if the Stars in Battledress were really worth their while, and my show was the one chosen to satisfy Sir James Grigg, the then War Minister.

It took place in Aborfield. I was duly told to put up a good show, for on the result rested the possibility of killing the whole idea of front-line entertainment.

Fortunately the Minister was impressed and the order was given to increase the establishment.

One day in conversation, G.B. told me that he thought I should be a revue comic after the war, to which I replied: "What did revue ever do for Sid Field?"

George said: "Who?"

Many months later he asked me again the name of the fellow I mentioned as a revue comic. I repeated the name, Sid Field and added that he was a marvellous performer. I remember his work in a show called *Red Hot and Blue Moments*.

G.B. said: "The old man has got him for a new show at the Prince of Wales called *Strike a New Note*."

Sid was brilliant and I was pleased when George asked me to write some sketches and material for him. Later, when Sid followed that show up with *Strike It Again*, he was taken ill, and I deputised for him three times in all.

On the last occasion, he was waiting to be taken home, feeling very bad, and we kept a look out for his car to arrive. When it did, it was the biggest, most affluent car I had seen.

"Is that your car?" I asked.

"Yes," he replied modestly. Then, like a little boy said: "Haven't I got on?"

One day during the war, he was driving that car with the window open when someone yelled in his ear: "Why don't you go dahn the bleedin' mines?"

Sid was so upset by this, that he bought an old taxi and for months afterwards he drove to work in it, leaving the other car at home. Very few pros will argue that Sidney Arthur Field was not a genius of comedy.

I was often recalled to London to bolster up certain other Army shows, and to assess the performances of some of the newer "comics". One artiste I liked was really "hamming it up" in a sketch I had written, and this was Arthur Haynes, who later became one of my Gang.

The good performers I made a mental note of, for in the back of my mind was an idea that later came to fruition.

I was always of the opinion that there was no such thing as an unsuccessful gang, providing it had the right leader. I fancied myself as the leader, because I knew how to write as well as perform my comedy.

I thought of Hughie Green and his Gang, Ted Healey and the Stooges, Duggie Wakefield and his Gang, The Crazy Gang with Bud Flanagan as their accepted leader, and all the other gangs, and I wanted to create a Radio Crazy Gang.

Whilst touring I set down the ideas, and in a tent before D. Day, I completed six half hour scripts of a very funny quick fire crazy show for radio called *Punchinello Parade* – Punchinello representing "comics" and "parade" stemming from the Army, in other words "Army of Comics".

I tried so hard to get a "Forces own show" but they told me to go about my business. Nobody wanted to even look at my scripts or hear my ideas.

D. Day was approaching. We, as an island, had been hammered a long time, and slowly, remorselessly, the long lanes had been filling up with miles and miles of tanks and jeeps, hidden from air observation, beneath the leafy trees.

The Americans were part of it all now, and troops were gradually massing around the ports of embarkation for the great offensive. I was sealed in at Southampton with both British and American troops.

I was, however, allowed the privilege of seeing the in-

67

vasion ships in Southampton Water. Thousands and thousands of ships, large and small, comprised the greatest Armada ever seen.

D. Day came, the combined might went into action, and shortly after, I found myself over there as a soldier and entertainer. We did shows non stop as they went forward from Normandy right through to Germany.

Ken Morris and I became a song writing team and we wrote many successful tunes together. I had already written three good songs that had been published since the war started, *Forget Me Not Lane*, *That's a Promise to You*, and *The Sergeant Major's Serenade*, and Ken was anxious to write a song for publication.

He came up with a tune at Southampton before D. Day and I wrote a lyric to it, which went something like this:

> There are miles and miles, of welcome smiles
> And oh, they're lovely to see,
> *Somewhere Within the Shores of Normandy.*

When, however, we did arrive in Normandy, we found our reception was almost hostile at first, so while the battle of Caen was raging, Ken and I, in a mud field just outside the battle area, re-wrote it.

> In an old world town, the moon looked down
> Beside an old water mill,
> and saw the fairest flower *on Primrose Hill*

Primrose Hill became a best seller.

Mud, mud, mud, it was everywhere. Thick, wet, slimy.

I was standing near a lake when the relief party arrived. It was the Arthur Haynes Party, he had been promoted to Sergeant and put in charge of a Stars in Battledress unit.

While I was talking to him, he pointed to a small slit trench filled with mud: "Blimey look at that," he said. "That's a trench!"

"I know it's a trench," I replied. "They're common around here."

68

"No, the mud I mean, look at it. You wouldn't get me in that trench for a million." I looked again and saw what he meant. It was alive with minute frogs, hundreds of them.

Just as he made his remark though, two Focke-Wulfs came out of the sky with machine guns blazing. Before you could say "knife" Arthur was in that same trench with little frogs jumping out of his ears and wide moustache. I have never seen anything quite so funny.

It's amazing how people react to a dangerous situation; when I looked up again I saw Tommy Nelson, in full battle dress in the lake swimming like an Olympic Champion in an effort to "get the hell out of there".

In the circumstances the first thing I did was to commandeer a black maria police wagon, and that was our transport for quite a while. In charge of my little entertainment unit, I had almost a free reign, at least for a time. It's true I had my orders, but sometimes according to troop movements it was not always possible to keep to our itinerary.

I remember at one place with a name like Lissioux, we called into a DDI (a place where you could stock up with tinned foods and spares of any kind). Here we loaded up with loaves and corned beef and when I asked where we might sleep the corporal said: "I wouldn't stay here if I was you Sarge, there's an outbreak of typhoid." I hurriedly got my lads aboard and drove on for a good many miles to a place called Bernay. It was there that the PLUTO (Pipe Line Under The Ocean) had been cut and twenty-seven thousand gallons of petrol flooded the surrounding area. Smoking was not allowed and with the petrol being red, it looked in places like a sea of blood. I had to house the lads in an old warehouse, that a few days before had been used as a German hospital. The Free French on liberation, however, had not been too forgiving with the Germans and my lads had to use the blood-stained sheets.

I had to occupy a windowless tiny cobbler's hut opposite, with all our gear. All alone. With the Free French creeping around, shooting first and asking questions afterwards, I wasn't too happy with my lot.

Being entertainers, we were always late returning to base and it was in the early hours that I was almost killed by a sniper's bullet as I entered the cobbler's hut. Thankfully it missed but it practically took the door off its hinges. I saved the bullet and have it now as a paper weight.

Another place we arrived at late one night was a large disused old chateau. We put the wooden shutters over the windows and lit candles. Len Marten slept on the billiard table (what remained of it) and in the morning he discovered he'd been bed companion to a huge bat. After we had searched the basement, printed matter showed the place had been previously occupied by the Gestapo.

A sense of unrealism came when we arrived at Middelburg in Walcheren, where eight out of every ten of our ships went down. The Dutch were delightful people and so happy to be liberated we could do no wrong. At least, that is what I thought.

Being the Sergeant in charge, I was the only one to carry a revolver, and when we arrived in Potterbakkersingel in the early morning I saw two Germans walking towards us.

I wondered if we had travelled too far, and was about to draw my gun and fire when something stopped me. I'm glad it did. They were Dutch boys. Having been deprived of food and warm clothing for three years, as soon as the Germans departed they had raided the warehouses and store rooms and put on anything to keep warm.

My lads were billeted with a young married couple and I was next door with some older people and their big son. He spoke English very well and was interpreter for us during our stay. On the first morning I was asked to share their breakfast, which they could ill-afford. I accepted because otherwise they would have been insulted. The meal consisted of black bread with some brown sort of sugar and they said prayers before and after it.

I decided to make up for their generosity.

Later that day I bribed the cook sergeant of the nearest Army place and he loaded me with long loaves, tinned butter, tinned meat, tinned jam. When I staggered back to them late at night with this lot, I shall never forget the look of delight on their faces, it was three years since they had seen any food like it.

I asked them to share it with the people next door, who were housing my lads, and between them they opened the tins – even cut their hands in the excitement – and then, because I asked them to share, they got out a pair of scales and with a lump like an egg in my throat, I watched them weigh it.

Some of the Dutch Islands were still occupied and the enemy was only a short boat trip away. As we did our shows to the lads we noticed that the front-row audience were all dressed ready for battle with camouflage in their hats and blackened faces. We got used to seeing someone creep in quietly and silently beckon toward the first two rows who would unobtrusively and reluctantly withdraw. While the show continued, they would raid an island occupied by the enemy, do as much damage as they could, and then return, sometimes before the show was over. When they returned to their seats I found myself mentally totting up how many had not returned.

It was a strange war for me. My mind often went back to the time when I was in the West country, back home, and I had received special instructions to "Proceed forthwith to Bulford Barracks, Tidworth, Salisbury Plain, and you will entertain the new Allied Supreme Commander General Eisenhower."

Together with a charming young singer Celia Lipton (Sidney Lipton the band leader's daughter) and an Army Show Band, I was there to "Top the Bill". The memory of that event lingers, for the first speech the General made in this country was to that audience of British and American serving men. He said some very nice things about the show

and concluded with ... "We have shown Cheerful Charlie
how much we can laugh. And now we're gonna show the
British Nation how we can fight!"

To travel between Vlissinger (Flushing) and Middelburg
one had to drive carefully by the side of a canal and the
journey had to be completed in a certain time before the
water level increased and flooded the track.

The main road had already been flooded when the dykes
were opened and I recall that we were half way down the
track when we were confronted by another vehicle and
there was no room to pass. I nipped across the grass verge
to see what other route there was, if any, and suddenly a
voice called out: "Stand still Sergeant, you're in the middle
of a minefield!"

Only me and my laundry man knows how nervous I was!

It was a strange experience, for even after the war, if I
crossed a green sward at the side of the road to answer the
call of nature, I still had that feeling of dread.

Standing naked with the lads and washing our pants out
in an old petrol tin was commonplace, but at Lion sur Mer,
we had a shock; we had been sleeping in an empty house,
but it wasn't until we left that we were told it hadn't been
cleared for mines.

As we were entering Germany and the war was virtually
at an end, I was flown back to London. My wife was in
hospital. Our baby was lost and she was on the critical list.

I was then ordered to report to Sloane Square, where I
was given an office. There were dozens of new faces waiting
to go out in shows, and I had to write them. Funny solo
routines, sketches, comedy songs. Research into the classics
for the straight musical men. Auditions of the new performers coming in. Officers would suddenly arrive at my
room and tell me to drop everything and concentrate on their
show. There were so many new officer producers I didn't
know where to start.

One young fellow came up to my room and said he was
told to report to me.

"What for?"

"They said you'd fix me up."

"Well what do you do?"

"I sing comic songs with the ukelele!"

"Oh, good, well what sort of comic songs do you sing?"

"Well, they said you'd write them for me."

"O.K. well I'll sort something out for you, and you go and get your uke."

"I haven't got a uke!"

"Christ, you'll be telling me you can't play one in a minute."

"I can't . . . they said you'd teach me!"

Downstairs in the great hall, the performers would stand and sit around waiting to be chosen for an outgoing unit. The Tanner Sisters, those two talented ATS girls, are two that come to mind. An officer would pick seven of them, usually three girls and four boys. They were picked according to their type of talent and the officer producer would find a title for his show and then come to me for material. It was then rehearsed, kitted out with costumes and props, and sent out to the various outposts. France, Germany, Italy, India, wherever in fact, there were troops who needed entertainment.

I was nearly off my rocker churning out all the material at times, but it was great fun. But it was difficult to blend Army "bull" with crazy comedy.

A particularly objectionable lieutenant came to me one day and said, "You will drop everything to work on my show."

Having several "priority" jobs on hand I had to get permission to drop everything else. I was informed that the officer in question must wait his turn, which didn't please him, and he felt the whole thing was my fault. When it finally came to his turn, he told me that his show was going to be called *Futuristic*. Fine I thought, not much of a title, but if that's what he wants, OK. "Yes," he went on. "You see the show opens with a cop directing the traffic

73

THE WORLD IS FULL OF CHARLIES

in a *helicopter*!" I explained as gently as I could that
he would find that very difficult to do on a NAAFI counter,
which is where you sometimes had to do a show. Having
toured all the gun sites, fort walls, and underground ammunition dumps, I could speak from experience. This was
his second set-back and he began to storm at me that I was
unco-operative. He reported me to the Colonel and when
he was told of the reasons for the argument, he blew his
top and told the officer to go away and come up with a better
idea.

This made me even less popular. The lieutenant did
come back. This time with a new idea, and a fresh load of
sarcasm for me. "... and I don't care what you say Sergeant, this time you'll do as I want."

"Yes sir. What exactly did you want?"

"I want some very funny opening couplets to fit this
situation. You see the show is going to be called *Auditions*."
My face must have fallen.

"Have you any objections?"

"No sir, I was only thinking that auditions are what are
given before you are approved of. It's almost like saying
'beginners' or 'on approval'. Not what I would call a good
catchy title, sir!"

The roof nearly went off.

"All right, sir. I'll do what you want. It's your show."
I tried to placate him.

"Right, well the back cloth is going to be a blank wall.
In the middle there will be a stage door and the idea is that
they are all lining up outside to go in and do their audition.
Before they disappear through that centre door though, they
nip down to the front of the stage and sing a couplet about
what they do – a comedy couplet to get some laughs."

"I see sir, then they go through that door and off stage
after they've each done their opening bit?"

"Yes, that's right."

"Yes sir, so that the climax to the big opening impact
is an empty stage?"

I was hauled again to the Colonel and this time I had a go.

All this time I had kept the six scripts of *Punchinello Parade* that nobody wanted.

The BBC arrived and told the War Office that they weren't happy with things. The *Merry-Go-Round* series on the radio had two hit comedy shows: *Much Binding in the Marsh* was the RAF's, with Stinker Murdoch, Kenneth Horne and Sam Costa and company; and *Waterlogged Spa* was the navy's, with Eric Barker, Pearl Hackney, Jon Pertwee and company. The Army had George Melachrino and a vocalist. The BBC wanted a comedy show to rate alongside the other Services.

I was sent for. "Sergeant Chester, you will write a *hit* comedy show for radio!"

Now there's an order for you! "Yessir. Permission to speak freely, sir."

"Granted. What is it?"

"I'd like to do this sir, providing that I submit the scripts to no one but you and the BBC. Any interference from some of these 'producers' and I'll get nowhere. And sir," I added, "I insist that I am top man and that I have the company I choose."

"All right."

I knew from experience who I wanted. I wanted to present a show that had something of everything; I wanted the fastest comedy on the air. I could tell the solo jokes, that was my speciality. Then there was Arthur Haynes, the plump funny "ham" I had seen and met so many times before; Ken Morris, the best piano entertainer; Len Marten the straight man, who could not only do "voices" and accents. but could also do a sophisticated solo joke; Ramon St Clair, the vocalist; and Frederick Ferrari, the tenor.

Frank Chacksfield was the backroom boy musical arranger, and we were to have the Blue Rockets Band under Eric Robinson.

I now went back to my six *Punchinello Parade* scripts

and rewrote them to suit the boys. I knew the best lines for each one. I had them in a room every day for three weeks with a mop stuck between two chairs.

"Now that's the mike fellas ... in out ... don't get in each other's way. Right now, off the top again."

The top brass sent for me.

"Now Chester, this radio show, you realize that you won't be earning anything from it, the money must go to the PRI funds."

"Yes, sir."

"Yes, well you can have two guineas, to cover any out of pocket expenses, but the rest goes to the Army. Oh yes, and you realize that your brain belongs to the Army. I'm afraid you'll have to assign the rights, title and interest of the show over to me, otherwise you can't go on the air."

I knew that if I signed the rights, title and interest over to anyone, I would not possess my own show, even if it was a success.

I stalled for time. I told him that the rights of the show were held by my publishing company.

"You'd better get them released then, hadn't you?"

"Yes, sir."

I went to the publishing company, which Reg was now running, and used the office stamp and, at the same time, I signed my half of the publishing company over to Reg for one shilling.

Next, I handed the paper over to the Colonel.

I Hereby assign the rights, title and interest of
the show *Punchinello Parade* to........
It was dated and stamped as released from the
Victory Music Publishing Company.

My next move was to belt round to the BBC and change the title of the show to *Stand Easy*.

It meant, of course, that there was no show under the *Punchinello Parade* title, and at least I had retained my own brain child.

It was a hit from the word go and was the first show to supersede the listening figures of ITMA, the record-breaking war-time Tommy Handley programme. Leslie Bridgmont was our producer and friend. A man with a great sense of humour and yet who could smile inwardly and retain a sphinx-like exterior, a thing that worried me for quite a while.

The first time I took my scripts to him I watched his face, and with hardly a smile he went through them. My heart sank. Then he would say: "That's fine old boy. Fine!" Then he would permit himself a grin.

At last, the show that nobody wanted was on its way.

I had made sure that it included the right boys. There was only one girl included, and her name was Louise Gainsborough. How she kept pace with my lads I'll never know, but she certainly held her own.

We became a must for Forces and civilians alike, and our "Down in the jungle, living in a tent, better than a prefab . . . no rent" is still quoted some thirty years later.

Murdering a song at the piano. Time marches back. The back-to-front Planet. Interviewing a Statue. Tarzan of the Tapes.

I pulled all the ideas I could think of.

As the show gained in popularity the war was in its final stages. The BBC asked me if I would do a "civilian" edition of the show when I was demobbed.

Of course I would. I could see a way now. If I could stay on the air a little while longer, my name, with my Gang, would no longer be barred from the Moss Tours, they'd *have* to have us.

To make sure that the public got to know us for certain, I had posters made including my newest idea: *Whippit Kwick*. They were posted all over London stating that Whippit Kwick intended to enter their homes.

I then had several thousand small cards printed with a big thumb print on it, bearing the words "Beware. The mark of Whippit Kwick". On the reverse side was advertising the time and date of the show due on the BBC's Light Programme.

I bribed the man at Olympia, where literally thousands and thousands of demob suits were hanging, to let me take my time over my choice and the ten shilling note worked wonders. I was there nearly all day stuffing these printed cards into all the pockets of the demob suits.

I often wondered what the thousands of men did with the cards they found in their demob suits but I do know they reached Scotland and Germany.

> *It's better to pick a flower for*
> *someone living,*
> *Than light a candle for someone dead.*

CHAPTER FOUR

If peals of laughter are the milestones
on your journey – depend on it, you'll
never get lost.

By now my Gang and I were firm favourites with the
listening public. The show went on the air from week to
week, with repeats on Saturdays. We had a ten-year contract
with George and Alfred Black, and on one count, we
totalled twenty-eight thousand fan letters in fourteen weeks.

One of the first fan letters I ever received in appreciation
of *Stand Easy* was from a young, dainty looking girl, who
attended every show. She could have passed for a school
girl. Her name was Eileen Tavner, and such is the way of
fate that after moving away from London to Kent some
twenty odd years later, I met her again, when I was opening
a local Scout fete. She was then Mrs Brinkley and being an

excellent shorthand typist, she has been my personal secretary ever since.

When, at long last, success came, I opened an office in Lisle Street, engaged a secretary, a shy young girl called Rene, who had plenty to put up with from the Gang and myself. Somehow she kept us all at arm's length and I used to know whether my scripts were any good by watching her type them. I would watch for the smiles on her face as she typed.

I also had a man called Charlie Murray to do the odd jobs and errands – an Army mate of mine who was one of the singers in the concert party, "The Craziliers". It was through Charlie's misfortune that I wrote a hit song during the war. He was from the Dalston area and while we were still rookies in Newtown, one of the first bombs to be dropped on London killed a number of his family, including his mother. He was given a week's leave. When he returned he was, naturally, a much changed man but one can't turn the clock back and I was anxious to try to bring him back to some sort of normality. He loved singing in the shows, but he swore he would never sing again.

I told him I understood how he felt but that I had written a song especially as a tribute to his mother; surely he wouldn't refuse to sing that?

He was so overwhelmed that he agreed. The song was the solo part of a large "presentation" and had the finishing line:

> . . . then I'd have your picture *Mother*
> smiling at me . . .
> *If I could paint a memory.*

I changed the word MOTHER to ALWAYS for publication purposes, and it became one of the big songs of war time.

Another of my Army war-time pals walked into my Lisle Street Office one day. He was an eccentric dancer, who had been through ballet school. He was one of my Stars in Battledress crew who went with me after D. Day right through to Germany. What a character. A man with a most cutting wit and who later scored a measure of success as "my man Jeeves" in my TV Shows.

Eric Carnell Grier was anything but a success after the war. He told me that he had invested all his Army gratuity and savings in a show at Weymouth and had lost the lot. He was washing dishes for Lyons Corner House when he came and asked me if I had a job for him.

I explained that with Rene the secretary, the odd job lad, and Charlie Murray, I was more or less fully staffed.

He replied: "I'll sweep the floor for £4 a week!"

After all we had been through together, I couldn't do anything else – I just handed him a broom. In no time at all he became my personal manager and worked for and with me for over twenty years.

There were times when he had to be suppressed though, for his wicked sense of humour was a little strong at times. For instance, when I played the Chiswick Empire (this time as top of the bill), I received a call from a woman and her daughter Barbara, who had been writing fan letters regularly. They came to my dressing room and I found that conversation was heavy going, because between them, they hadn't any. It resolved into a series of questions from me and a simple "Yes" or "No" from the mother.

The daughter just sat there and although quite sweet, she had the biggest feet I had ever seen on a young girl. I'm certain that she could have got a job stamping out forest fires; they were enormous.

After ploughing on and getting more depressed than ever, Eric arrived and weighed up the situation in a flash. He said hurriedly: "Oh by the way, I've fixed you both up in the front row and I think we ought to get you settled in your seats." He took them down through the pass door.

The door itself was a big iron thing and you had to go down two steps, and whereas mother got through all right, the daughter stumbled and left one shoe behind. Immediately Eric said: "Don't bother dear, I'll get *two* stage hands to pick it up for you."

I took Eric with me practically everywhere.

The BBC were doing a broadcast series called *Variety Ahoy* and I was booked to do a strong solo patter routine. At the time I was driving my left-hand drive Buick car. When we arrived at the quayside to board the liberty boat which was to take us to the aircraft carrier HMS *Indefatigable*, all the other artistes and the producer were waiting for us. The Stargazers, who at that time were probably the best known of all the vocal groups, shouted to us: "Come on Charlie!"

They saw us get out and lock the car, and must have thought that Eric was driving, for the normal driving seat would be on the side he had occupied. We ran to the liberty boat and amid the chatter during the journey, I forgot to introduce Eric as my personal manager.

The show was an enormous success, for the Navy are a superb audience and if there's one thing I do know, it's how to handle a service audience. Eric proved a very popular back stage entertainer and the Navy lads took to him well.

I noticed in the Navy, however, that they are very "deck" conscious. It's "upper decks" and "lower decks", and although in the Army it is "officers" and "other ranks", the division in the Navy seems a little more marked.

We were feted afterwards by the Captain and the officers in the wardroom. This was an enormous room, almost like a dance hall, and the babble of conversation from the men and their wives and guests, was such that one had to shout to be heard.

The charming Captain's wife dutifully made her rounds, chatting to all concerned, and she must have asked who the young man was standing alone by the door. It was Eric. The Stargazers said they weren't sure, but they thought he was my chauffeur! Being a menial he was ignored for a while.

Eric saw me look up from the autographs that I was signing and I said: "Are you all right?" He nodded that he was, but I could see that he was fed up and feeling a little out of things.

Finally the Captain's wife relented, she walked over to him and amid the babble shouted to him: ". . . and what do you do?"

Of course, it had to happen. Just then the conversation seemed to die and there was almost silence as Eric shouted his reply, and all that was heard was: "Do you mean sexually, or socially?" Every head in the place shot round and the poor woman went all the colours of the rainbow. She tried to make it seem casual and went on. "I mean, what are your hobbies?"

Eric, with a stony face replied. "Tiddleywinks!"

Because of his earlier ballet training, Eric was quite poetic in his movement, almost to the point of effeminacy, and quite a number of people got the wrong idea about him.

I remember saying to him: "Eric, why don't you smoke a pipe, it's far more masculine?"

"I will if you will," he said.

We both bought a pipe and I smoked some tobacco called Gold Block, which was very strong. He decided to wait until he found a more mild tobacco.

One day in Simpsons, Piccadilly, I reminded him about the pipe, and he produced it, shining and new, from his pocket and walked over to the kiosk situated in the centre of the great store, right in the middle of all the surrounding departments.

The woman with the Grecian hairdo was a fine saleswoman and put on a wonderful act.

"Can I help you sir?"

"Yes. I'm looking for a mild pipe tobacco."

She eyed him up and down, looked very coy, pointed her finger at him and said: "Mild pipe tobacco . . . yes."

She then turned her back on him and went through a whole routine of tapping different shelves muttering: "No, I don't think so, possibly," and finally, "Ah yes!"

She then handed him a packet. We both looked at

her choice and it bore the name "Parsons Pleasure".

Eric looked at the packet in silence, then at the woman and then back to the packet again. This went on so long the woman felt she had to say something, so she enquired: "Is something wrong?"

In a voice that could be heard from one end of the store to the other he replied.

"No dear, I was just looking for a row of choirboys' arses."

I have never seen a woman look quite so shocked.

For a young man, he could often act like a testy old man, and once in the Moo Cow Milk Bar the conversation went something like this.

The grey-haired old lady serving us: "What can I get you?"

Eric. "Two coffees please."

"Yes, certainly, black or white?"

"White please."

"Yes, cream or milk?"

"Oh milk please."

"Strong or weak?"

"As it comes."

"With sugar or without?"

"Oh for Christ's sake give us the coffee, not the recipe."

I was once asked to give prizes away during a big dance in the Midlands, as a celebrity. Eric came along and as soon as we arrived, I introduced him and he was handed a sherry. Then I was taken to the prizegiving in the hall and Eric was left alone.

Cracking a few gags and giving the prizes took some time and when I finally managed to get back to the starting point, Eric was still standing there with his drink.

"Is the sherry all right?" asked one of the officials.

To which Eric cuttingly replied. "Yes thanks, do you buy it by the barrel?"

Magnanimously the man then said, "Now would you all like to go and enjoy the dance?" Whereupon he pulled the swing doors open revealing all the dancers on the floor. Eric said, too loudly for my liking, "I say, C and A have done awfully well, haven't they?"

This was Eric. He could get away with murder. What he could, and did say and do, to the Tiller girls, any other man would have got his face slapped for.

They were somehow quite content to just say: "*Eric!*"

Strangely enough, although he was stage struck, he was always very nervous in front of an audience. You only had to click your fingers and he would sieze up on stage, but it was one of those blank spots followed by an embarrassed laugh, that made him a celebrity in his own right as "my man Jeeves".

This came about in a show I devised called *Take Pot Luck*. It was the first ever give-away show on TV and in it I had dancing girls, give-away girls, Len Lowe, the best straight man in the business, acts, and, of course, Jeeves. My leading lady was changed from time to time and I had just discovered a girl called Edna Fryer, a very funny young girl with a good comedy sense.

We were doing a sketch I had written about the Khyber Pass, in which I was a spy, and the girl was Delhi Nellie (a comedy Mata Hari). We were sitting in the Indian Night Club passing the information and on the table was a great Hookah pipe, which I had to smoke. Eric was the Indian servant and for this he had blacked up and had to leave his glasses off. We had ordered two glasses of milk, which the prop boys made up from washing powder, and when Eric served them minus his spectacles, he didn't see the Hookah pipe on the table, consequently the tray lopped over as he stood it down and the two glasses of slippery washing powder spilt over the stage where the dancers had got to work.

Something had gone wrong and it could only mean one thing, Eric went blank. He couldn't think of a line, instead he just kept bowing and scraping saying: "Oh effendi . . . oh effendi."

Not being fed the right lines I couldn't do my next lines,

so I ad libbed and by now the studio audience were in hysterics.

"Stop bowing and scraping then. You look like G. H. Elliot on another farewell tour."

"Yes effendi."

"Well if that's all you can say you'd better get back to your hovel in Putney."

"Yes effendi." By now he was panic stricken and all he could do was laugh.

"You'll be stamp collecting next week."

"Stamp collecting, effendi?"

"Yes, unemployment stamps."

How we finished the sketch I'll never know, but I kept saying that he would have to go. Within a few days, however, letters began to pour in saying "Please don't sack the laughing valet."

I naturally built on this and actually wrote in things for him to do wrongly. We would have a spare 21-piece tea set as well as the actual prize so that he could trip and smash it by accident. I even wrote one sketch in which something went wrong that wasn't his fault and when I agreed that it wasn't, he leaned on the wall in relief and *the wall fell down*.

The studio gags came thick and fast.

Tawny Neilson once said to me: "Charlie, can't you pull a joke on Alan Clark, your announcer?"

No sooner said than done. This was in the days when all broadcasts were "live". Alan, I noticed had a habit of holding his script with both hands one each side of the mike and reading it at arm's length, standing with his legs bent.

I suggested to the lads that while Alan was announcing: "It's look out for laughter in the next half hour, for here's Cheerful Charlie and his Gang", we could make sure that laughter was heard from the studio audience.

It was a planned movement, one would lift up the announcer's jacket, the others would undo his braces, I would make sure that his shirt was held in position, and then, down with his trousers!

The place rocked – especially at the end when he had to pull his trousers up to walk away from the mike. It looked so incongruous for a BBC announcer. Alan took it very well, and in fact he enjoyed the joke as much as anyone, and even now, years later, it is a talking point in the BBC. But in consequence, I received a letter to the effect that announcers must not have their trousers removed whilst in the course of their duties!

I told my lads. It said we mustn't remove them, but it said nothing about rolling them up. The next broadcast he not only had them rolled up but the hairs pulled out of his leg whilst announcing us.

A further letter informed me that we were not to touch the announcer. This instruction we obeyed, but danced Ring-a-Ring-o-Roses around him in such a way as to get our laughs anyway.

The powers that be at that time finally had my Gang and myself sitting with our backs to the audience until the announcement was over.

Anyone who has visited a studio show will be aware that behind the audience, the producer sits with the engineers behind a long glass window in a soundproof room.

The Gang were very quick to catch on if anyone of us started something, and at one rehearsal we started to "mouth" the opening chorus, pretending we were singing with gusto and yet making no sound at all. Then, as soon as the engineer came out of his room into the actual studio we'd be giving it all the voice we'd got. He spent quite a while dashing up and back testing out the microphone to find out why it wasn't working before he tumbled to the joke.

In those days we had two "effects men" and they had to make all the noises with whatever implements they could find and these "effects" were all done in full view of the studio audience. They constituted a great part of the show itself. A guaranteed laugh was to watch a long tumbling crash take place with four of five chairs placed on top of each other and a bucket full of glass chippings at the side. The chairs would be kicked over, the bucket grabbed and rattled almost immediately, then a dash to make a door slam and perhaps a siren whistle. The effects men certainly worked hard and to see them "sticking to script" was real comedy on its own.

The jungle chants that were so much a part of my programme, were a novel way of introducing a topical event in gag form. These were so popular that at one time, I had bookmakers ringing me up to mark their card what the subject was going to be. I wouldn't have told them, and I couldn't anyway, for they were the last things I wrote before we went on the air. I even had a petroleum company in Southampton ring me up and tell me that in three weeks' time they were going to strike.

When Bruce Woodcock was fighting an important international fight, I had a short wave radio on in the studio and three chants ready. One for if he won, one for a draw, and one ready in case he lost the fight.

He won, and we were able to chant:

Big Bruce Woodcock, what a wicked hound
He's been and "done" the Frenchman – seventh round.

Bruce's manager, Tom Hurst was so knocked out with the fact that we had beaten the BBC News to it by a matter of minutes, that he sent me a wire later which read:

Woodock's manager thought you might
Like to see the next Bruce Woodcock fight.

I accepted, and it was a marvellous night for me. Apart from being in Bruce's dressing room before the fight, I watched him knock out his opponent just as a wag in the audience yelled "Come on Bruce! Whippit Kwick!" And he did.

Bruce himself was so enamoured with these "chants" that he asked me to write some which he could recite to himself when doing his roadwork. I don't know if he ever used them but I often imagine him putting the actions to:

> *Jab with the left,*
> *The right one too,*
> *Cover up and let him have it ... ONE, TWO!*

I have always had a great affinity with boxers. Men who can stand up and really hurt each other and then, at the sound of the bell, walk over and shake hands. The boxers I have met may not have won awards as academicians, but they have certainly been amongst the most sincere and generous people I have ever known. Strangely enough, although serious about their work, most of them have had a good feeling of comedy running through them. Freddie Mills was a great character, and to this day I will never believe that he took his own life.

Another man I was particularly fond of was Randolph Turpin, the World Middleweight Champion for all too short a time.

I was at the ringside when he beat Sugar Ray Robinson, and standing on the chairs with excitement the entire crowd were shouting themselves hoarse – even Dorita, my wife, and she is not normally that demonstrative. Suddenly behind me we heard a scuffle, and with the excitement so intense a man dropped dead. It turned out to be the brother in law of Jack Solomons, the boxing promoter.

I spent many happy hours with Randy, riding horses for Bob Butler's stables up in Warwick.

Horses have always featured largely in my life and there's not much I don't know about them, for in Eastbourne, my Aunt Nell had connections with a huge hunting and hacking establishment. She lived above the stables, and my brother and I used to help to clean out the stables, polish the brasses, dubbin the leather and harness. Even as tots George and I used to take them down to the sea and many are the hours I spent walking one up and down whistling to it to make it urinate. This is something they find difficult to do when suffering from certain ailments and whistling to the animal encourages it to do this.

If they had the gripes, we used to swing them in a hammock affair, because we were told that if they laid down with the gripes, they'd never get up again.

Taking two marvellous horses, Bonnie Hunter and Too Clever over the jumps with Bob Butler, I was able to tell him about how I learned to ride. My aunt, who was a character, used to wear a hobble skirt and sit side-saddle. She would make my brother and I ride in front, and apart from "posting" to change gait, if our behinds left the saddle, we knew it, for with a long stock whip she had a dead aim at our backsides and she would yell: "Daylight!"

Too Clever, my favourite horse at Bob's Stable, died not so long ago, at the ripe old age of twenty-seven.

Randy Turpin was a good horseman, and being a little hard of- hearing he almost looked apologetic at times. Except in the ring of course.

The boxing fraternity is filled with people that I have been proud to know. Could there be a nicer man than "Our 'Enery"? Henry Cooper was a tiger in the ring and he won my deep regard the first day I met him – he introduced his mother to me with the simple remark: "Charlie, have you met my mum?"

My hero of the ring from my younger days was the man who could do no wrong for me. I think I nearly wept when he got beaten, and it took me a long time to believe that he could be beaten, even on points.

His name was Len Harvey.

I remember the time when I made an after dinner speech for Jack Solomons, at the World Sporting Club, all the greats of boxing were there, including my idol, who sat almost opposite me. I cracked one or two gags, of course, and in a serious moment I told Len about my earlier feelings. When, a little while later, I went to his table, I said: "Of all the people you did fight, who was the hardest, Len?"

He turned and said: "This bastard sitting next to me." It was Jack Petersen. How nice it was to see these great veterans of the ring, sitting there together, having given each other bloody good hidings.

One of the craziest and yet gamest fighters I ever saw was a man known as "Nosher Powell". He was a man with red hair who was so funny in the ring, and yet so hard, that Jack Solomons always booked him to close the bill, because the other fighters found his contests hard to follow.

It was during a prize-fight, after dinner, that I sat next to George Raft, the American film star. He was a boxing fan himself but when we met again I discovered we had another mutual interest. The gaming tables. He was in London to be mine host at the Colony Club, and I have an interest in the casino bearing my name just off Piccadilly.

Shortly after one of these fight evenings, he went back to America only to find that he was barred from returning. He was broken hearted I know. Having sat with him on several occasions, one paper reported that I had taken over from him for the purpose of training croupiers for the Bahamas. There was also mention of the Mafia being involved. What rubbish!

I have always, and often to my regret, liked the atmosphere of the gaming tables, expecially roulette. I used to stand for hours watching the counts and countesses in Monte Carlo, the quiet apprehension and good manners of it all fascinated me.

I have played in many casinos myself, Tripoli, Italy, Monte Carlo, Portugal – but the only place I really won at – and this may seem hard to believe – was Las Vegas.

It was during my second visit to New York. I went to Goodman and Todson, the quiz kings of TV, I had a panel game which I felt would interest them, and after chatting our business I found myself wandering all alone around New York.

Although it's a fascinating madhouse of speed and hustle, one can get terribly bored all alone.

I had certain friends over there, but they were working and I felt it unfair to take up their valuable time, willing though they were. I saw that George and Bert Bernard were doing their wonderful miming act there. Some time before they were with my shows at the Opera House Blackpool and the London Palladium. I had to drop in on them. They were overjoyed. They even introduced me to their audience as a "great comic from England", after which I was invited to do the Ed Sullivan Show.

We had many suppers together at the fish bar on Broadway with Johnny Ray, and although we shared a lot of laughs I told them that I was cheesed off. I said I thought of flying down to Vegas.

Bert, who was married to the lovely Zoe Gail, exclaimed that Las Vegas was where he had made his home and that Zoe had recently been on the phone saying she needed some money. Would I take a packet down to her when I went? Of course. Phone calls were made asking Zoe to meet the plane and to fix my accommodation.

She phoned back to say she'd had a hell of a job to fix me up and they asked if I were a big gambler.

"The biggest in England," she told them and I was in, then instructed me to "act it up Charlie. You're a big gambler, don't forget."

I did. I lit up a long cigar and strutted around like a Mississippi River Boat man from way back. The only thing was that I stuck out like a sore thumb with my terribly English well-cut suit, collar and tie. All the others were in cowboy attire or jeans!

I stood aghast at the sight of the hundreds of slot machines in the foyer of the hotel, not to mention the wheel of fortune by the door and the crap games. The machines ranged from the nickel jobs to the two-dollar machines. These are where you insert a dollar in two machines that work with the pull of one handle. If you are fortunate enough to win both jackpots, the chances of which must run into millions to one, you get not only both jackpots, but two thousand five hundred dollars also, which is the only paper money you will see. They do everything in small change so that the machines are constantly fed. If, however, only one jackpot comes up, you get whatever drops, plus two hundred and fifty dollars paper money.

I am as great a sucker as the next man for slot machines anyway, and after fiddling around with the smaller machines I suddenly realized that I was supposed to be a big gambler from England. I made my way to the two-dollar machine.

Following me around were two young married couples and when I won a jackpot plus two hundred and fifty dollars, I could hear them excitedly say: "Jeez, watch the Englishman." I then made my way to the roulette table.

They have separate colour chips for each player there, to eliminate any arguments about whose chips are whose. Mine were white.

"Come on, let's watch the Englishman," I heard the quartette say behind me.

I modestly put a chip on zero, noticing that they also have double zero, which is a bit of a take on. Then another on eight, and another on twenty-six. These were my numbers.

Number eight came up right away, and as the croupier shoved chips towards me the chorus behind me got more excited. "Jesus! Look at the Englishman."

It came to me again that this was just messing about and if I was being watched as a big gambler, I was pretty pathetic.

I put quite a few chips down. Zero, eight and twenty-six.

Twenty-six came up. As the enormous pile of chips came my way the chorus went wild and I began to feel a little too conspicuous. I began to sweat with embarrassment. I was alone with no one to talk to.

I tried to act as though I was just amusing myself. I looked at the great pile of chips in front of me, I was loaded down with the heavy dollars and I had two hundred and fifty dollars in my back pocket.

I thought I might as well look as if I could gamble, so I now took a very large handful and placed them slowly on zero. Another large handful on eight and a further large amount on twenty-six.

I couldn't believe it when he called zero.

Now I had an ocean of chips in front of me and I wished that I had a companion to talk to, so that I could share the embarrassment of having to leave the table after only being there for such a short time.

There was no one, except the dawn chorus behind me.

I played foolishly for a while to make it look good, and when I cashed in I had won enough to cover the entire holiday. Then it was back to work.

The Gang and I toured the halls, the Moss Empires for two years, and seeing my name headlining, after all I had been through, made me feel good.

I must confess that, in a way, I found it rather frightening when I saw the mounted police keeping the crowds in order. I realized all too well that our popularity was not only because we were a gang of laughter makers, but that we were all ex-soldier lads, who had broken through from the rough to the big time.

I often hear about today's pressures and I have to smile, they aren't new, they've always been there. Ever since I was accepted as a national "name" there have been pressures of every kind. Apart from having to write the shows each week for radio until the early hours of the morning, as well as do the tours and live inside a suit case, I was now expected to open garden fetes, judge beauty competitions, read the lessons in church, appear at charity functions, police concerts, road-safety campaigns, visit hospitals, prisons and so on.

These things by the way, have never stopped, so when they talk about pressures, I just don't understand what they mean.

It's obvious that some can stand up to the strain of popularity far better than others, for sadly I recall that some very good friends of mine like Peter Waring, Tony Hancock and Robert Moreton, ended their own careers far too soon.

Robert Moreton was a strange man, you may remember his great gimmick was his "Bumper Fun Book". He had a *penchant* for large ladies, in fact the larger they were, the more he loved them. In one particular radio series he was a co-star to Hattie Jacques, and though she was probably unaware of it he followed her around with dog-like devotion.

We were playing one particular town and our landlady said: "I've got Mr Moreton coming next week." There was such pride in her voice as she said it.

"You won't offer him meat will you?"

"Pardon?"

"You won't offer him meat will you? Only he's a strict vegetarian and the very thought of eating meat, he'll be as sick as a dog."

The landlady was grateful for the information and said she would remember. I believe that by the Thursday he was shouting: "For God's sake can I have something decent to eat. I'm starving!"

One of the favourite gags of the Gang was the cork gag. This was devised by the Bud Flanagan's Crazy Gang and consisted of a champagne cork, which had one bulbous end and a flat end. We used to push a long pin through the stem diagonally, so that the point would come out at the centre of the flat end, and then bend it over. Then we'd pick a stooge, make sure that his attention was occupied, and then we'd gently hang it on the front of his fly. It was so light that he didn't know it was there and it looked for all the world as if he was exposing himself. We tried it out on Ramon St Clair, the singer, and he couldn't understand why the Tillers smiled when they walked away from him.

I devised another little joke which had a marvellous effect. Because of our success with the jungle chants, and remembering that people did not, at one time, recognise us by our faces, we would find a large restaurant or cafe and seat ourselves at different tables, pretending to be complete strangers. We had rehearsed the thing so well that it went like clockwork.

Regardless of the strangers that would be at our individual tables I would shout: "*Tom!*" followed by Arthur Haynes. who looked up and shouted the same thing. Then from another table Ken would repeat it loudly, and the same thing from Len Marten. Following this in rhythm we would do the pay off in unison, so that the whole thing sounded like . . . "*Tom . . . Tom . . . Tom . . . Tom . . . pom tiddley om pom tom tom.*"

We would all then continue eating our food as if nothing had happened. Heaven knows what the other customers thought.

Leslie Noyes, who took over from Henry Lytton playing my late Colonel Rodney, was very fond of double talk. He was never quite up to the standard of Stanley Unwin, but nevertheless he fooled many people.

Arthur was a little upset one day and said that *he* wanted to do the joke, so Leslie and I went into a pub where he had a drink and I my usual lemonade. It was on a Sunday morning. The place was empty except for the two of us and the landlord.

Half way through the drinks Arthur came in, stamping his feet all over the floor, muttering some gibberish like "Gunz ge felta mitta broygen . . . Iss darven ze cloom?"

The landlord with perfect English asked: "Wass ee say?"

Leslie ignored the landlord and spoke to Arthur.

"Mitzi mavanno Czechoslovastardbar?"

"Ja, ja . . . Gunz ge felta mitta broygen zaga?"

Leslie turned to the landlord and explained. "He says he's a Czechoslovakian parquet floor expert."

"Well tell 'im I don't want no bleedin' parquet flooring. This is a pub."

While Leslie and Arthur kept up the farce the landlord kept giving me the eye to slide further down the counter, which I did, and he whispered to me: "I can't stand bleedin' foreigners. Tell him to get rid of him and we'll have a drink together."

I relayed his message to Les, who quickly said some more gibberish, to which Arthur replied. Leslie seized his opportunity.

"Oh what a shame . . . he says he's got to go now!" Poor Arthur couldn't argue about it, so he played it up by shaking hands all round about three times and went.

No sooner had the door closed behind him than the landlord rushed over and locked the bar door.

"I can't stand bleedin' foreigners," he said again. Then: "Now boys, what'll you have?"

We stood for quite a while chatting with him and when we got outside poor Arthur, who hadn't even tasted a drop, was soaked to the skin. It had been pouring with rain and I had locked the car.

Another joke we pulled was because of Arthur's great laugh – a high pitched infectious sound. I suggested he went into a big department store in Liverpool, where they had comic and funny books laid out on one counter.

Arthur was just to look at the comics lying there without touching them and start to laugh. I would go over to him and start laughing at him. Then Ken Morris would laugh at me, laughing at Arthur, and Len Marten would add to the chain. Before long we had the whole of the store laughing like demons, and none of them knew what they were laughing at.

It had been a long time since, in my early days, I had gone to see the Crazy Gang at the Palladium. In their dressing room Bud cleverly worked it so that wherever I was, I appeared to be in the way.

"Look, tell you what little Charlie, you stand over there by the door, you'll be all right then."

I did as I was asked, not noticing the rubber pipe concealed just above the frieze, nor the cleverly hidden water can rose, just above where I stood. Bud went to wash his hands and connected it and Charlie boy got the lot. I was soaked, and although the lads didn't know it, in those days it was my only suit.

They all belted on to the stage to do their bits, all except Teddy Knox, who softened a little at the sight of my being soaked. He said, "That wasn't very nice was it? Perhaps we should teach them a lesson." He then got on a chair and made small punctures all the way along the piping.

I wasn't there when they next pulled the gag, but Teddy tells me that they all got saturated.

Time had marched on and now my own Gang pulled one on me.

I had fixed them all up, plus some of the speciality acts, in the same digs. The woman had written to me saying she was a famous landlady for pros, and they lived in White-ladies Road, Bristol. Seeing from the advance publicity that we were to be there, would I confirm who would be staying with her. I affixed the letter to the noticeboard backstage, and those who wished to stay there signed it. This was then sent as confirmation to the landlady.

When we arrived in Bristol, about seven or eight of us, headed by me, staggered with our bags up the pathway in Whiteladies Road.

The door was flung open by a portly Jewish lady, who flung her arms open wide to me and exclaimed: "Welcome. One of us!" I didn't want to disillusion her so I said nothing, except to return the pleasure of our meeting. She stood in the hallway and spoke to the company.

"Now you'll all be very comfortable. This," she said, pointing to a long room, "is the breakfast room, and this," opening a door opposite, "is the lounge. There are toilets and bathrooms on all floors."

She assigned a room for each of us and then explained. "I shan't worry you. My husband's a jeweller and we live in the basement. Hettie will look after you!"

Hettie, bless her, was the grey-haired retainer, four years older than God, and when she carried a plate of soup to the table, you only got what was left after she'd finished spilling it.

After our first meal there, I went out to do some shopping, and from that moment onwards, every meal for me was purgatory. Each time Hettie served me anything, she kept staring at my neck. She would slowly walk round the back of me looking at it with deep concern. If I noticed her doing it she pretended that I'd been mistaken and wait for a further opportunity.

Every course, every meal, this happened and I began to wonder if I'd got a permanent tide mark. It began to get on my nerves. In fact it ruined the week for me.

It wasn't until some time after I learned that during my shopping expedition after the first meal, she must have said to one of the boys what a nice young man she thought I was.

They replied: "Nice young man? Young? He's sixty-eight!"

"Oh don't be so ridiculous," she countered. Whereupon they insisted that I was indeed that age and that I'd had my face lifted three times. They also added: "If you look closely on his neck, you'll see the join marks!" I have laughed about it many times since, but it certainly was a damned uncomfortable experience.

As I said earlier, when once you become a "name" it opens up wide vistas, for many and varied are the things you are asked to do.

Charity shows and garden fetes seem to be the permanent musts. I have performed so many opening ceremonies and my admiration always soars for those people who, year after year, spend so much time to prepare one of these functions. They have to try and book a good "name" for an opening ceremony and then praying that the weather will be kind enough to make it a success.

An amusing episode happened at one place where I was asked to judge the ankle competition, I agreed and was taken to a series of long screens, which had about two feet of space between the bottom and the ground. Behind these screens were a long line of females, and all one could see of them was the lower end of the calf, the ankles and shoes.

This meant that no pretty face could influence. I was judging the ankles only. I did the judging very conscientiously. Then I came to one set of legs in gun metal grey stockings, the seams were rigidly straight, the legs were lovely, and the matching grey shoes made her the winner.

I tapped the lady's legs and said that this was my choice and would she now come round to the front of the screen. She did. She was enormous and waddled round to a laugh from the audience that was quite embarrassing.

I only ever judged one baby competition, because I discovered it was the best way to lose friends. Every mother rightly thinks her baby is the most beautiful which is only natural but some mothers won't forgive you if you don't pick hers the winner.

But I have always had a way with kids though, I don't know exactly what it is, but I can get a kid to do almost anything for me. A most poignant moment for me concerning a child was at Chipperfield's Circus.

I was playing at Coventry with Richard Hearne (Mister Pastry). Richard happened to be a great friend of Dick Chipperfield, and was asked if he would clown around at a special Christmas Show, to an audience made up entirely of children from homes and orphanages.

One of my shows on TV around that time was *Pot Luck* and Dick Chipperfield asked if I could devise a special give-away programme for the children. The big prize being kept a secret. It was an adorable, tiny, Shetland pony.

I was told that some nuns had brought some very pathetic children to the show and they were pointed out to me. They also pointed to a tiny dot of a girl and said, that at the slightest encouragement, she would sing. She was the youngest in the orphanage. At the end of the fun-and-games part of my performance in the ring, I walked over to her and

asked if there was anyone who would help me, and true to
form she agreed.

As we stood in the centre of the sawdust arena I said:
"I know, we'll sing *Gentle Jesus* together, as it's Christmas
time." To which she replied: "Oh no we won't we'll sing
Away in a Manger."

"Of course! That's an even better idea," I said gladly,
realizing at the same time that I could only remember the
first line.

I pitched a key and we started. Thank the Lord she knew
it well, and as I petered out, there was this tiny little mite,
in the centre of the ring, singing to a packed house, and an
audience far bigger than she knew, for the whole country
was watching on television.

A storm of applause greeted her finish and I knelt down
to her level and told her it was surprise and wishing time.
"Now what you have to do to make a real wish come true,"
I explained, "is to kneel down like this, and then put your
hands together, just like praying, and then close your eyes
and wish, but you mustn't open your eyes until I tell you."

She did so and silence fell over the great crowd. I backed
away softly from her, leaving her entirely alone in the pose
of prayer. Wishing. Backing away to the entrance cloth I
watched her. She never moved. Then I led in a tiny pony and
a great "Aahh" went up. Still she never moved. I brought
the animal up right behind her and it was actually breathing
down her neck. When I finally told her that her wish had
come true and she could open her eyes, she expressed her
joy as only a child can do . . . When told it was hers to take
back to the Home, she was unable to believe it. And then,
as I lifted her on to the pony's back to head the finale
parade, I noticed that there was not one dry eye in the place.
Even the TV cameraman was weeping and Richard Hearne
was sobbing his heart out . . . and so happy.

It's strange how, in a life of laughter making, sadness can
play a large part. Even more strange, is the way things have
a habit of coming back at you, years later.

We never knew, for instance, just how many lonely people listened in to us, and after hearing us so regularly on their radio sets, accepted us as their "family", or part of it at least.

One lady sent me a pound note, saying would I buy the boys a drink, as she felt that she knew us all. She explained that she was unable to get about because she'd been badly burned. I couldn't send the pound back, and at the same time I didn't want to take her money, so I put some to it and bought her a bouquet of flowers, which I sent her.

Then, after a time, her letters stopped coming.

It was many years later, when I was guest artiste for the Bebe Daniels and Ben Lyon show, *Life with the Lyons*, that I got a surprise. We were all invited after the show, to a private room above The Captain's Cabin, a favourite pub of the BBC artistes. Assisting with all the eats and drinks, was a very charming woman who said: "I wonder if you remember my mother? She was the lady in Notting Hill, who you once sent some flowers to. She must have thought the world of them, because after her death the flowers were still in the vase. She never threw them away." I realized then why her letters had stopped, and I now realize just how much the gesture meant to her.

Among the thousands of letters I received, one in particular is still remembered. It was from a Brigadier VC who had written from the jungle in Bechuanaland.

I must first explain that part of my show was a strip cartoon in voice and sound, which was really a take off of the famous Fitzpatrick travel talks. I called it the *Amazing Adventures of Whippit Kwick*. In this, I created various "characters" and referred to the general public as the "natives". Whippit Kwick was the cat burglar, Anne Cuff was his girl friend. There was Humpty Go Cart the tough guy; Sarah Nade, the jungle songstress; Bwana Wash, the native soap salesman; Dan Druff the jungle barber and his dog Shampoodle; Ray Ling, the Chinese Fence; and Stabu, the elephant boy. We always referred to

Stabu as speaking in his native tongue, which Len Marten did in his rankest Cockney accent. The elephant's name was Forsythe, which was a leg pull on one of the largest men in show business, Charlie Forsythe, of Forsythe, Seaman and Farrell.

When Stabu spoke to the elephant in his native tongue, it was usually to say: "Git up there Forsythe yer perisher . . ." Whack!

The Brigadier, in his letter, explained that he had been on Safari and had got hopelessly lost when a boy on an elephant came on the scene. The Brigadier was able to converse in his language. The young lad told him the right directions and terminated the conversation by whacking the beast across the head and shouting: "Git up there Forsythe yer perisher!" Apparently a group of soldiers had taught him to say it – the only English he knew.

It's funny too how people were incensed over innocuous jokes. It led me to a deep study of humour, on which I have since lectured at schools and colleges. In retrospect, this in itself gave me a great sense of achievement, for I left Stonhouse Street School in Clapham, with a school leaving "reference" which was a guarantee to keep me out of work for life, had I shown it to anyone. It simply read:

This boy is always late. Has brains but will not use them. A constant urging and driving is necessary.
Signed H. Launder (Headmaster).

But by the process of trial and error, I began to realize that no two people were the same; what was funny to some, was unfunny to others, which meant that it wasn't possible to please them all. I realized after a while, that there is no such thing as a sense of humour, it's an emotion and of all the emotions in the human body, humour is the most fickle.

I heard a good joke the other day . . . I wish I could remember the damn thing! How many times have you said that? Yet you will remember some stinging remark you didn't like.

People, I discovered, are emotionally concerned over a great many things. Workmanship, religion, politics, loved ones, physical defects and so on. This came to me forcibly when doing a routine with Arthur Haynes in my radio show. I happened to say: "That's a lovely shirt you're wearing Arthur. Do you send it to the laundry, or do you tear the buttons off yourself?"

I had a letter, written in furious terms, from the head of a laundry in Streatham, saying: "We don't tear buttons off, we take a pride in our work."

On another occasion I joked, "My brother has been very ill and the doctor told him he must sleep in the open air, so he joined the Police force!" Before I was off the air, I had a policeman from Edgware Road ring up and shout: "You can do my bloody night duty any time you like!"

Soon after the war, when we still had to queue up for petrol coupons, had bread units, and orange juice was rationed along with meat. Mr Attlee was then Prime Minister, and I made my usual topical gags about the situation.

"All this queueing up for bread and petrol, meat and stuff . . . things wouldn't be like this if Mr Attlee were still alive." Some people asked me if Mr Churchill wrote my scripts after that one.

My only answer was to follow it up the next week saying: "Last week I was a bad boy, I said a joke about Mr Attlee not being alive . . . and he heard me. He jumped up, looked in the mirror, and boy, was he relieved!"

Some people get too emotional over such jokes and it dulls their appreciation of something funny – or at least meant to be funny.

If, out of one hundred men in a room, one of them was deeply in love with a bow legged girl, and I cracked a gag about the subject – something like: "That girl was so bow legged, when she pirouetted across the stage she looked like an egg beater!" – it's odds on, the one who wouldn't laugh would be the man in love with the bow-legged girl. He would have taken it, not unnaturally, as a personal thing.

Humour is not only a deep subject, but also a delicate one and because of over emotionalism, I suffered badly in Belfast.

My show had been on the road, touring all the big halls, for nine months, and naturally in those days we had been passed by the censor, plus the fact that most big cities had their own "watch committee".

It was fine until we had to appear for three weeks in Belfast. After the first show, the management usually came around to tell you if there was anything in the show that might offend the locals. No one came, and I naturally presumed that all was well. But when the local paper came out someone had written a letter complaining about the disgusting contents of the show. I couldn't understand it. I had no guide as to which gags offended. I pruned the whole show down as much as I could, and wrote to the paper asking whoever it was to come and tell me which part had caused the offence.

Ten days later, I discovered it was a young school girl, who's objection was to a Girl Guide sketch, in which I hoisted a pair of drawers up a flag pole!

But there are rewards. I received one when a national press "Opinion" quoted something I said. It came out of a speech I gave at a very large school. I was told that after presenting the prizes I would be expected to make a small speech, and then ask the headmaster for a half holiday for the children. This, of course, ensured my success.

What to say in a speech though, had me puzzled. I couldn't tell a string of gags. I knew very little about the school itself, but in conversation with one little lad, I mentioned Hitler, and the boy said: "Who's Hitler?" This astounded me, for we hadn't long finished six years of misery because of him. The lad did, however, know all about Henry VIII and all about his wives and sexual appetite. My speech therefore was about this little lad, and I said that I thought History should be taught backwards. In other words, what happened last year, ten years ago, twenty and so on, going back to Boadicea. At least when leaving school they would then have some idea of what was happening in the world, and it wouldn't matter if they weren't sure on what date the Romans pitched their tents in Colchester. I felt that with history taught in reverse they would at least know why we fought the last war, and the one before that.

The old pros used to say: "Never perform with kids or animals, because they always steal the show." But I've worked with both, however, and derived many a laugh from them.

I think the most outstanding of the animals on the bill with me was an act in one of my Palladium shows. It was an almost human chimpanzee called Marquis, who worked with his owner Gene Detroy; the rapport between them was fantastic.

Just before going on to do his act, he would bring Marquis to my room, and although it didn't seem strange at the time, this childlike animal was included in the conversation as if he understood every word.

I always knew if he had behaved himself on stage and performed well, for afterwards I would hear Gene saying what a good boy he was, as he carried and cuddled him all the way back to his dressing room at the top of the building. If he had not worked well, I could tell by the grunting and the thumping of little feet, together with the cursing of his master, as he was scolded and made to run up the stairs under his own steam.

Most of us would stand in the wings and watch the act. Marquis acted like a human. Gene would get him to pedal a scooter, and if he didn't go fast enough Gene would say: "Hurry up son, here comes an agent." More often than not, the animal would blow a raspberry in return. Another trick they kept in was when Gene saw a small hole bored in the stage and said: "If you look down that hole, you'll see the girls dressing," and the animal took pains to look down it.

One part of the act was preparing for bed, in which a cot was brought on to the stage and a baby's potty placed underneath. The animal then had to kneel and say its prayers after which he reached for the potty and sat on it before retiring.

George Black was worried about this last trick being included in the Command Performance. "We can't have the thing sitting on the pot in front of the Queen, Gene. It's not the thing. Is it possible to delete that trick?" he asked.

"Oh it's all right guv'nor, don't worry about it, I'll tell him not to do it."

"Don't be so bloody daft. It's all right saying you'll *tell* him not to do it, but after all it's a chimpanzee and I don't want to run the risk of offending Her Majesty."

"Don't worry about it Guv'nor. I promise you he won't sit on the pot," said Gene.

He was far more convinced than G.B. was.

During the act on the important occasion, G.B. stood in the wings and I stood next to him. He was more nervous than I had ever seen him before.

"I hope to Christ he doesn't sit on that pot," he said to me.

"Gene must know what he's doing, G.B.," I replied, trying to reassure him. Then it came to the part where the cot was dragged on the stage, and the hurried whisper to Gene was almost frantic.

Gene laughed. When Marquis kneeled down to say his prayers all went well, but then, suddenly, the little brown hairy hand shot under the bed and pulled out the potty.

G.B. closed his eyes. Gene hissed at Marquis. "Don't you *dare* sit on it!"

The monkey looked at him with brown questioning eyes.

"Don't you sit on it, or I'll give you a belting!"

107

Suddenly he moved as if he was going to sit as usual, then he picked up the chamber pot and rammed it on his head. George Black breathed the biggest sigh of relief I have ever witnessed.

Marquis had two other chimpanzee pals and Gene adopted another one, a baby, which they named Cheerful Charlie, after me. This now made a stable of four. Marquis, Baron, Charlie and one very large chimp which Gene called "Stupid". Apparently this one wouldn't learn anything and was not very playful.

They were housed in Gene's dressing room in four cages two on one side of the room and two on the opposite side. This left an avenue between. Arthur Haynes went up to the room one day and was speaking to Marquis, which meant his back was turned on the cage housing "Stupid". Whilst Arthur bent forward to talk to Marquis, this other brown monster's great hand shot out towards Arthur's rear, and gripped him firmly.

Arthur, large though he was, gave a squeal like a stuck pig and ran for dear life down the stairs. I can't say I blame him.

Another animal I became fond of was a white horse called Snowball. I used her in a sketch at the Palladium, and she was the most intelligent and affectionate animal I have ever worked with. We would stand in the passageway at the back of the stage waiting to go on, and if I forgot to give her her ration of sweets or apples, she would give me a nudge in the small of my back that would send me flying.

When I remembered her titbits, however, she would stand behind me and munch with her head on my shoulder.

She was used as the tag line to the sketch. I was the butler and an escaped convict, and the last lines of the sketch were: "My Lord, the mayor is without . . ."

"Well don't stand there . . . show the mayor in."

Whereupon I would open the scenery door and bring in the mare.

Long before this, there were several gun shots, we also

used to fire at the picture on the wall of a battleship, and even that too would return the fire, so the whole scene was a bedlam of noise.

The gunshots didn't worry our large horse; she just waited to be led on. This, however, could have been unnerving, for immediately after the shots, the door was flung open, the bright lights hit her, and as I walked her on, the audience would yell and start to applaud. Almost immediately the black out came to signify the end of the sketch, and then, in the darkness, the great tabs would be drawn and hit her up the backside. It's a good job she was good natured and placid.

We retained this old horse when we played at Finsbury Park Empire.

For this show each night she had to be walked from Paddington, where she was stabled, to Finsbury Park, and she was timed to arrive at the opening of the show.

We opened, and some time later I was informed that although the horse had arrived, they couldn't get her in the theatre. To do this she had to pass down a tunnel leading from the pavement straight on to the rear of the stage. She was too tall to go down the tunnel. They tried for over an hour to pull her head down and make her go down the dark tunnel, but it was no use, it couldn't be done.

By now the sketch itself was under way, and whilst performing we had whispered conversations as to how we would end the sketch without the horse.

"When I say the Mayor is without, you say, 'Which Mayor?' and I'll say the Mayor of Bucharoff. Then you shout, 'Well tell him to Bucharoff back again.'"

No sooner had we arranged this than it was time to start the shooting, and although they had been trying all evening to get old Snowball down that tunnel, as soon as she heard her cue, the gunshots, she ducked her head and stomped her way down on to the stage and made her way ready to go on.

I shall always have a soft spot for that old horse.

I have always been grateful for a fairly quick mind, and I've been able to hold my own with most people in repartee. In this particular field, the two great comics I have admired for so many years are Ted Ray and Tommy Trinder; there are none quicker at ad lib.

Tommy created a classic example when he was doing cabaret at a night club. His catch phrase was "Trinder's the name ... You Lucky People!" Orson Welles, who at that time was just divorced, happened to be in the audience and didn't seem impressed with Tommy, and when he started "Trinder's the name ..." he got no further when Orson Welles shouted: "Well why don't you change it?"

In a flash came the reply. "Are you proposing?"

I used to think I was quick with the comebacks, but I realised that someone in the gallery can be just as quick – if not quicker. This was proved to me at the Metropolitan Theatre in London's Edgware Road, where I saw an artiste who was brought over by Jack Hylton. A man known as Harry Kahn, the mental marvel and indeed he was.

The finale to his act was to be strapped by each ankle and hoisted upside down against a great blackboard. He would then write down something he was reading, whilst quoting any well-known poem suggested by a member of the audience. It was usually *If* by Rudyard Kipling, or *The Green Eye of the Little Yellow God*, or some such classic. To open his act, however, he would, as a quick throw away, hold a small blackboard in front of him and bend over it with a chalk, and explain that he would write three long words, which he invited them to shout out. He would then alternate by writing them upside down, the right way up, forwards and backwards, whilst at the same time pronouncing them in reverse order. Which was indeed a feat.

He called for long words and received many variations. On the Wednesday, however, he asked in the usual way: "Any long words please."

"Saskatchewan."

"Saskatchewan, yessir, upside down and forwards."

"Another long word please."

"Mississippi."

Then came the usual response. Then, looking up: "Another long word please."

From the gallery a single word was called.

"Rubber."

"That's not long enough!"

"Well *stretch* it!"

The place fell about, and so did I, but it did teach me to beware. Other people can be just as quick, just as funny, and it was a lesson worth remembering.

One of the hardest ad lib jobs I had to do, was for the BBC. Remember that broadcasts were "live" at the time, and only the purest of material was allowed. I was doing a series called *Midday Music Hall*, and I was resident compere. This took place at midday at the Aeolian Hall, New Bond Street – not the best place in the world for comedy.

At ten to one, when the show was nearly over, I had my eight minute spot to do, plus the closing tune and credits and that would be it. The phone in the hallway rang and I was told hurriedly that a sketch by a film star in the *Henry Hall Guest Night Show*, just starting at the Playhouse, was so bad they had deleted her from the programme and would I stand in immediately after I'd finished my broadcast. It meant I would have to ad lib for seven minutes.

I finished mine at exactly one, a taxi was waiting, and I had to work out a seven-minute top-of-the-bill spot in the time it took to get to Northumberland Avenue. That was a tricky one, but fortune smiled and I got away with it nicely. As a result Henry Hall and I became such friends.

Henry was always the "gentleman" of the band world. We decided to have a friendly feud, the same as some of the American stars. I would crack gags about his age, and he would do the same about my jokes.

This was fine except for a couple of things, one was the fact that as a comic it was easy for me to make jokes about him, I had the advantage, gag-wise. So, to be fair, I had to write his comebacks as well.

The other snag was that so many listeners wrote in saying that it was a pity that two such "nice" people were at logger-heads. They really believed the feud was genuine. We derived a good deal of fun from it before we finally decided to drop the idea.

One season, when I was at the Opera House in Blackpool, Henry Hall, together with a great cast of names, was play-ing at the Hippodrome, a little further down Church Street.

As the Gang and I had just one twenty minute break in the show, I decided we would invade their theatre. Charlie Murray, my ex-army mate who was my right hand man off stage, walked down the centre aisle with a banner which read on one side: THEY'RE LAUGHING AT THE OPERA HOUSE and on the reverse side as he turned it: CHEER UP AND HAVE A DRINK WITH CHEERFUL CHARLIE.

He went right down to the orchestra pit and stood with this banner and with the Gang all dressed in white aprons and chef's hats, including our gorgeous leading lady Edwina Caroll, we dispensed drinks to the audience from prepared trays. We had ready mixed gins and tonics, whiskys and sodas, beers, cigars, and within the space of less than a minute they had all gone. Sid and Max Harrison who were on stage at the time, wondered what the hell was happening and thought for a moment that they were getting the bird.

After the initial shock, however, they joined in the joke and the band busked my signature.

I blew a whistle and shouted: "Back to work Gang," and as we withdrew from the theatre, Henry Hall walked on to the stage with a look of disbelief on his face and shook his fist at me as we departed to a storm of applause.

I might have guessed he would get his own back. In my show I was doing a sketch called Cheerful Charlie Matthews. A football sketch in tribute to the great Stanley Matthews, the wizard of the dribble, who lived in Blackpool. I was the sloppy footballer being trained by Arthur Haynes. At one point he'd shout: "Right, now we'll give you the sandwich."

I'd reply: "I'm not really hungry."

"No, not that sandwich, a football sandwich. OK boys! Sandwich!"

Two of the others then ran on and barged me from either side in a perfect sandwich, knocking all the wind out of me, after which Arthur would scathingly say: "Put your backbone behind the ball."

At this I would put my hand up my jersey at the back and withdraw a horrible rubbery spine, which I would lay behind the ball, followed by a spineless walk, and so on. Then we got to the foul. After being fouled I would have to lay on the floor and wait for the magic sponge. It was important that I didn't see this happen: I was supposed to be groaning in agony. Then the trainer would run on with a bucket of water, lift my jersey in front and slap the soaking sponge on my belly.

The management were very considerate about this and to ensure that the water was neither too hot nor too cold, they had two buckets, one with boiling water and one cold, which just before use would be "adjusted" so that it was just right.

I was in position on the floor, not looking, and I wondered why the delay, but suddenly a whole bucket of water, not just the sponge, was emptied over me.

It was Henry Hall in full evening tail suit, who had secretly arranged it. After emptying the bucket over me he took a quick bow and went.

What he didn't bother to do was temper the water, he just picked up the first one to hand, which happened to be the hot one and I finished up like a boiled lobster.

Happy memories are the legacy of
good fellowship.

CHAPTER FIVE

Christian Fellowship is the bridge
between those who are known to WANT,
and those who want to KNOW.

ONE of the ideas that formed part of the *Stand Easy* show on radio, was the Harmony for Hospitals spot. This was really a vehicle for the boys to be able to sing a straight song in corny, but homely harmony. I also wanted people in hospital to know that we recognised their plight, and that this was their special spot. The idea was for me to mention lots of names and give messages from loved ones and then, finally, the Gang topped it with a particular song to fit the occasion.

This brought in mail by the shoal.

But after a while the BBC asked me to delete it, for at that time our show was broadcast by the General Overseas Service. It is a complicated thing to understand, but the

115

Light Programme, as it was then, would sell its shows to the Home Service and vice versa. Any of these purchases, of course, meant repeat fees to the performers, which was an added pleasure.

The BBC felt, however, that I was mentioning too many names and the Harmony for Hospitals spot was becoming far too "local", and this meant that places like Australia wouldn't be particularly interested.

They agreed that I should mention one name, and this gave me a problem. Out of the hundreds of letters for that spot, who could I choose? I racked my brains for an idea as to why I should suddenly only refer to just one patient, and after some thought it came to me. If film stars could win Oscars, why not sick patients – especially children?

I had some beautiful Oscars printed in the form of a citation, which were sent as a measure of encouragement in adversity.

The first Oscar patient was Leslie Judd, a boy of thirteen in hospital at Hammersmith. I had been informed of this lad through my secretary's fiancee, who was also a patient. He told us that the little lad had been paralysed for two years, and that he had recently walked two steps! Only two steps, but what excitement it had caused.

Having heard the story, I wrote to Leslie informing him that my "secret service" had told me about his recent achievements. I went on to say that we were considering him as our first Oscar award winner, and the following week he walked thirty steps. From two, to thirty! Not a bad effort.

I wrote to him again and explained that when he walked fifty steps he would be awarded with his Oscar. The following week he managed forty.

I again wrote to him, saying that I was delighted with his effort and that I was so certain he would walk his fifty steps, that we had decided to make him our first Oscar winner, with "honours". This meant that, by arrangement, there would be a radio on in his ward for all to hear, and as I mentioned his name as the Oscar winner, the local

116

Scouts group, waiting outside the ward, marched in with his scroll and, with due ceremony and salutes, handed it to him.

This made little Leslie feel very important, and after the award even the doctors saluted him.

It wasn't long before he walked his fifty steps and was discharged. Some weeks later, at my home in Finchley, I received a phone call from Leslie, who informed me that he was phoning from a call box near his house. He had walked there on crutches.

"My brother is waiting outside to take me home," he said.

After congratulating him and telling him how proud we all were, I told him that if it were possible, I would pay him a visit on Christmas morning. I hastened to add that it wasn't a promise, for I had already given my word to visit Kathleen Bullock who was a patient at Whipps Cross Hospital. This poor soul had been on her back for twenty-seven years, completely crippled with arthritis.

The phone went quiet for a second, and then a voice said: "Mr Chester, if you'll pay me a visit at my house on Christmas morning, I'll throw one stick away!"

I promised there and then to be at Number 37, Stringer House, Nuttall Lane, Bermondsey, on Christmas morning.

I visited Kathleen, who, because of her infirmity, had photos of all the "stars" pasted on the ceiling, for that was the only way she could continually look at them, and while I was there I was asked to visit all the other wards. They all wanted me to pop in on them.

This is something that I would dearly love to have done, but it is an enormous place and it would have taken me the best part of a day.

I therefore had to ask them to forgive me and promised that I would return some other time. Nurses and walking patients, however, barred my exit and refused to let me go. But I explained that if I visited young Leslie, the other side of London, he had promised to throw one stick away. Suddenly I found they had made an avenue for me to go. It was an extremely touching moment. I hated to leave them but a promise was a promise and I drove from there to the down-stairs flat of the great block.

My large Buick car caused quite a stir and I could hear some of the kids standing around saying "Someone's come to see Leslie."

When Mrs Judd opened the door, she beamed at me and said: "Come on in, I know who you are!"

Being Christmas they offered me all manner of drinks, but I settled for a cup of tea, and after chatting to the family in general for a while, I turned to plump little Leslie, who was sitting by the fire with his two great sticks leaning up against the fireplace.

"Well Leslie," I said. "I've kept my promise. Now, what about you?"

He was silent for a moment and he looked at me steadily. "Would you like to see me walk without sticks?" he said.

At that time I went there hoping he would attempt it with just one stick, and here he was, offering to walk unaided, just because I had paid him a visit. There was a look of expectancy from his mother, father, sister and brother.

"Would I? Now that would make my Christmas," I told him.

He seemed to struggle with his thoughts for a moment, and then having made up his mind, he rose from the chair, and as the family made a gangway for him, he walked across the room, right past the kitchen table to the door and continued up the passage to the front door. He then turned and started to walk back to us, looking straight at me for approval. When I say "walked" it was a stagger, but at least he did it under his own steam.

His mother had tears streaming down her face, the family themselves could almost be heard breathing and I had a lump like an egg in my throat. I just had to keep talking or I think I would have shed a tear myself.

He insisted on doing a "dance" with his mother, for an encore. If there is such a thing, that was one of the saddest, happiest moments, of my career.

The story, however, doesn't end there. Afterwards I said to him: "Now that you can walk Leslie, I'll tell you what – the day you walk up the fifty-two steps to my office in Wardour Street unaided, I'll give you anything you ask for!"

"Anything?" he asked with a laugh.

"Yes. Anything."

Some months later, on a Friday, the phone rang and a voice said, "This is Mrs Judd. I've got Leslie downstairs, he wants to come up only he's afraid you might think I'm pushing him from behind!"

"Come on up then," I replied.

Mrs Judd came up first, and a little later there was a clomp, clomp, as Leslie made his way up these stairs by himself. What an achievement! It took me over an hour to discover what he really wanted more than anything else, he was too embarrassed. It was a movie camera.

Now fate is a funny old lady, I had recently been to America and while I was there I had bought myself one. I had since used it once only – to take pictures of my baby son Peter – so it was virtually brand new. It was delivered to him on the Saturday morning.

This, however, was still not the end of the story.

I had to go with my show, for the summer season, to Blackpool, and during our run, we also had to continue the weekly *Stand Easy* broadcasts from there. These were recorded at the Co-op Hall.

I received a phone call from a hospital in the Midlands, saying that they had a patient who was in a bad way. He kept asking them to get in touch with me. His name was Leslie Judd and he had a tumour of the brain. He was due to have it removed on the Wednesday morning, and the chances of his recovery were only fifty-fifty.

I explained to the surgeon as much as I could about Leslie, and with some of the facts to hand, he agreed that he would have a radio on, very quietly, at the boy's bedside, at my request.

I spoke to Leslie, through the broadcast, and said: "This week's Oscar winner is our number one award winner, Leslie Judd." I explained that he was to have a brain operation the following day and that he was going to show us all, how he would not only have the operation, but that he would come up smiling.

He did. He later wrote to me again 'apologising' that his legs had gone back on him and that he wasn't able to walk again.

I paid him a further visit, and he presented me with a cigarette box that he had made for me. I keep it and treasure it to this day, for shortly after that, he died. Without doubt Leslie Judd was one of the bravest little boys I have ever had the privilege of knowing.

It was about this time that Noel Whitcomb, writer for one of the national newspapers, wrote a cutting article about the *Chin-up* magazines I had printed, which we distributed to all the hospital patients who wrote to us. This gave them stories of the Gang, what we were doing, all about our shows, articles by the individual members of the Gang, joke pages and so on.

Noel took the bother to count the number of times my name was mentioned in the magazine, which I paid another Fleet Street journalist to edit for me, and Noel wrote an article saying that Charlie Chester was Charlie Chester's number one fan.

To get him to answer the phone was difficult, but when I finally did, I told him I didn't mind what he said about me, "but please don't 'knock' the Oscar idea, as it's working miracles." I am grateful that he was content just to knock me and not the Oscars and they went on from strength to strength.

The Gang often went with me to various hospitals and we would clown around and serenade them.

Arthur Haynes and Ken Morris were particularly good with children, and what some of those nurses and matron had to put up with from us was enough to make them blush.

120

Soon I had people from all over the country recommending other patients for Oscar awards. I sent out literally hundreds of them.

When I played Pantomime in Manchester a woman called on me and told me that some time before, I had sent an Oscar award to a little girl called Margaret Grindley, who was then in Crumpsall Hospital. Would I go along and see her as she would like to meet me?

Margaret was unable to walk. To reach her I had to pass through a long ward occupied by about eight or ten ladies. At the end of their ward was another, smaller one with a half-glazed roof. I remember my first impression being that it resembled an artist's studio.

The nurses had been busy. Margaret sat in a wheelchair by her bed, and she had this smaller ward all to herself. She wore a pretty dress and had a pink bow tied in her hair. Her legs were about as thick as my wrists from ankle to thigh and they were encased in irons. I bounced in and started chatting as if I'd known her all my life, instead of it being the first time ever.

After a while, my conversation was directed solely to the sister and one nurse, who stood by the bottom of the bed. I told them I was going to write a book about some of the Oscar winners and in particular, about boys like Leslie Judd, I told them how he had walked for me and they were quite impressed.

"Oh yes, Leslie walked all right. In fact, I'm sure Margaret would walk for me, but it's such a lot of bother with those extended arm things," I said casually.

"Well I don't mind!" The sister said.

"And I don't mind," the nurse followed up.

Then a small voice behind me said: "Well, I don't mind!"

"All right then, let's give it a try, shall we?" I suggested.

The nurse went quickly and returned with some long extended metal arms and the sister and I helped Maggie up from the wheelchair. Young Margaret then, with the aid of these crutches, walked slowly, step by step, towards the larger ward, where she was greeted by the older women patients, who couldn't believe their eyes.

Maggie was watching her own feet with fascination as she plodded slowly along, and the nurse made a remark that I shall never forget. She called: "Keep your head up Margaret, you'll never see the sun unless you have your head up!"

The dear little soul's head shot up and she looked straight in front of her.

"Come on back now Maggie," I called. "Don't overdo it, that's plenty for now."

When she was finally restored to her wheelchair, flushed and excited, I took the matter a step further.

"Now that you can walk Maggie, can I have the pleasure of the first dance with you at the Christmas Dance?" I asked. She blushed to the roots of her hair and said: "Yes."

Four days later, I received a letter from the sister saying that since I had asked her for the dance, she had been in the gymnasium each day trying her best to be ready for the occasion.

Then another letter came from Margaret herself, asking: "Would I forgive her if she didn't dance with me as she had got on so well that she was being sent home for Christmas?"

I wrote back and said I was delighted to hear how well she had got on, and that perhaps she'd let me have the honour at the New Year's Dance?

Another letter of apology came saying would I excuse her again as she had made such progress she was now being sent to the School of Stitchery and Lace in Sussex. That was the last I heard from Margaret.

I hope that she managed to walk normally, and that she found some of the joy of life that I discovered when I met her.

There was another young man who used to come and see me at Morecambe. He was always pushed to my dressing room and one day I said to him: "I hope one of these days instead of riding in like that, you're going to walk in here."

Several years later, the same young man walked in and said. "I told you I'd walk in on you!" I haven't played Morecambe since, but I'd like to think that if I did, my fan would walk in on me again, for truth to tell I am a fan of his.

One very pretty young lady wrote to me from Lewisham Hospital. She turned out to be such an avid fan and I learned that she had a birthday due. I went with the biggest bunch of flowers I could buy, and when she heard I was on my way up the stairs, she dashed into the lavatory and locked herself in. She was too shy to see me and in the end I had to leave the flowers on the bed.

I never did see Joan Treen, for sadly she died shortly afterwards of advanced tuberculosis.

At the end of my *This is Your Life* yet another young lady walked in on me as promised years earlier, only by this time she was a happily married mother.

I remember too a young boy whose mother ran a cafe to make ends meet. She wrote to me saying she was worried about her son because he was morose since his father's death at sea. The lad couldn't believe that his father had drowned because he was a champion swimmer. The mother thought the boy was under the impression that his father was alive, but didn't return because he didn't love them any more.

Her reason for writing to me was that the only signs of animation he gave was when my Gang and I were on the air. He had even called his little dog Whippit Kwick after my catch phrase.

I paid a visit and managed to talk to the mother before the boy got home from school. She told me that all he did was sit and stare into the fire and that he had no interest in anything. She also said that he was due to leave school following the summer holidays.

When the boy arrived, we chatted for a while and although he was distant and not very animated, I asked him to show me his dog, which he did. Then I asked him if he had anything else, to which he replied. "I have a monkey in a cage in the garden."

We went to see it. "That's a monkey and a dog you've got then, have you got anything else?" I enquired.

"Oh yes, I've got a couple of chickens in the back yard," he answered.

I don't know to this day what made me say or do it, but I put on an act and shuddered and said: "No I don't want to see those. I hate to admit it, but I'm frightened of chickens!"

He began to laugh.

I built on it. "It's all right for you, but it's terrible to have to tell anyone that you're afraid of chickens." I really convinced him that they frightened me to death.

"Come and see them . . . I won't let them get near you," he laughed.

Reluctantly I let him take me out to the back yard where, in an orange box sunk into the ground, covered by wire netting, there were these two small chickens.

I went through a whole act of being too nervous to go too near them, when he whipped off the wire netting and picked one up.

I nearly fainted with fright, which made him really laugh.

"They won't hurt you, look!" He cuddled the thing.

I called out to his mother. "Look at him, holding it like that! I couldn't do that if you paid me a million. But I'll tell you this, if I *could* handle chickens like that, I'd have a whole chicken farm."

Some months later I had a lovely letter from his mother saying that he had left school and had started a chicken farm and that he was his normal cheerful self again.

When I started the first of the tours with my Gang Show, we opened at Brighton and I received a letter asking if I would see a little boy who had just had one leg amputated. His mother informed me that he was having an artificial leg made, but she was afraid he wouldn't wear it, as it would probably rub and make the stump sore. Would I talk to him if she brought him to the stage door?

I went down to receive them and he sat in his wheelchair. He was about eight or nine years old and, clearly, a very sick boy. We got on like a house on fire and he promised me that regardless of anything he would be wearing his artificial leg by the time the show reached Brighton, nine months later.

Seven months later, however, I received a letter while I was playing in Sunderland, with a photograph enclosed of the little chap wearing his artificial leg and riding his bicycle. Two months later we returned to Brighton, but this time he was so ill he couldn't come to see me, so I went to his home.

He was dangerously ill and his mother was distraught. She told me that he had just undergone a further amputation, and suddenly in the hallway, she gripped me by the lapels. "You won't let my little boy die, will you?" she implored.

She showed me medical papers and told me what specialists had said. I talked to her gently for a while and tried to comfort her, but it was obvious that her son had no chance at all, because carcinoma secondaries were obviously all over his body.

"I have an idea," I said. "Let's both stand here a moment and say a prayer that he lives into the New Year, and then, if the Lord wants him, let him have him."

She agreed. The little fellow lived fourteen days into the New Year.

I only wish you could have seen his bedroom walls. He left behind some of the most marvellous drawings of Donald Duck I have ever seen.

Visiting people in hospitals and homes all over the country made me realise just how much the radio meant to them. The visits alone were all very exciting, and it was pointed out to me by the matrons of several hospitals that it was a talking point for days after. Although the staff do their best in so many ways, it is obviously routine work, and to a long term inmate, anything that breaks the monotony must be a good thing.

By the same token, those who have just arrived from their home environment and feel a little forlorn, especially children, are cheered immensely by the thought that "someone they feel they know" has called to see them.

This feeling of "knowing someone" through hearing them on radio has demonstrated itself to me so forcibly through the letters I have received.

I had one once from a dear old lady, who told me that her son was a guardsman at Buckingham Palace, and that he had recently left his wife. The dear old soul then wrote: "I want you to go to the Palace Charlie, and give him a good telling off, and he'll go back to his wife."

I could hardly see myself walking up to a guardsman and ticking him off, or that he would do as I asked, but I am sure the old lady was convinced I could.

With so many many letters of a similar nature, I couldn't fail to realise that I wasn't just a "comic" to those people, but a great deal more than that.

I have visited orphanages and homes all over the country, and my admiration soars for those "uncles and aunts" who dedicate their lives to looking after other people's offsprings. I associated myself very closely with two of these establishments, The Talbot Manor Boys Home, at Winton in Bournemouth, and St Winifreds Home at Rhyl.

My wife Dorita too, was always fanatical about kids; she would have been happy to permanently have a house full of them. She is also a very good psychologist with children. We have one son, Peter, having lost two others during the war. Nevertheless, the house at Finchley where we lived for seventeen years, was nothing if not full of noise.

We part adopted a young friend of Peter's. He had the intriguing name of Robert Burns. Bobby stayed on and off with us for years, and much later, when I performed in the play *Boeing Boeing*, in the Channel Islands, I was delighted to see him again. He is now a teacher, and happily married with a family of his own.

It was when I played Rhyl in North Wales that I first

visited St Winifred's Home – one of the many Church of England establishments for children of broken homes.

At that time, quite a number of them were absent as they had been offered holidays, leaving some tiny babies too young to go away, and five others: Raymond and Christine, a brother and sister aged seven and five respectively; Irene who was twelve; Christopher, eleven; and one other little girl. I was concerned that the five of them had been left behind with "no offers", so I asked if I could take them back to London and give them a holiday at my place.

The authorities agreed, and I promptly phoned my wife. She was delighted. Now she had something to worry about, and I could imagine her running about in all directions deciding which of the kids were going to sleep where!

It was a ten-roomed house, so there was little to worry about on that score. She took them everywhere. The zoo, the Tower, Hyde Park, boating in Regent's Park, shopping, Battersea fun fair. By the time they went home she was worn out, but had enjoyed every moment.

Irene was the problem child. Sitting next to a girl or my wife she was as good as gold, but sit her next to a boy and she was a terror. The nearness of a male would transform her, and I felt honoured to be one of the few who could put his arm around her without her bristling.

I saw Irene years later, when she was a sixteen-year-old receptionist at a hotel in Boscombe. I was invited to dinner there with Diana Dors, and when Irene greeted me with: "Hello Uncle Charlie," I could hardly believe it. Time works a miracle with children, especially girls.

Christine and Raymond, the brother and sister are both married with families of their own, and still write to us.

One of my favourite homes was the Talbot Manor Boys Home in Winton at Bournemouth. I first went there to help at their garden fete, and it was such a success that sufficient money was made to pay for most of the improvements they required. On my next visit they all turned out and lined up to form a guard of honour, with one of the tiny tots

127

blowing a cracked bugle. On getting out of the car with my leading lady from the show, one little mite was so excited he grabbed us both by the hand and said: "Quick . . . before you do anything else, come and have a look at our lavatories." They were the improvements the proceeds of the fete had provided.

I was able to help the Home in a roundabout way and started something which I hope will be copied by other counties. I used to go quite regularly to the Devon County Federation of Young Farmers, through my friend "Tug" Wilson, MBE. It gave me great pleasure to attend and do what I could at their Bath and West Show, Ox Roasts, County Dairy Shows, and similar events. In return Tug gave a few boys from Talbot Manor Boys Home a holiday. They also sent hampers for Christmas, and the children went back and eventually, two of the boys were adopted by the families with whom they'd spent their holidays.

These are only a few of the people I have had the pleasure of knowing, and when I look back over many years, and the hundreds of people in and out of hospital that have found a benefit of some sort through a complete stranger in the entertainment world, I believe that I was *meant* to do this job.

I realise that I never have been, and never shall be "everybody's cup of tea" but, to some, I have been both funny man, and friend.

It was fortunate for me that my wife did like children, and although, as I said earlier, we only had the one, our house was always full of them.

Having been a dancer for a number of years with the Rodney Hudson Girls, the BBC Step Sisters and the Victoria Girls, she agreed that when we were married she would finish with touring and devote her time to running the home.

War was declared on 3 September and three days later we were married. We spent our honeymoon in an Anderson air raid shelter and soon after I was conscripted. To help

Charlie Chester in the early days. (TV Mirror)

Charlie Chester pictured at the World Sporting Club. Bud Flanagan is his right.
(Matthews' News 8 Photo Agen

...arlie, in sparkling form, at a scout jamboree in Stoke. To his left, Stanley Matthews. ...taffordshire Sentinel)

...R H Prince Philip meets Past King Rats Charlie Chester, Tommy Trinder and Ben Warris. ...ooking on are Terry Cantor and George Martin. (J. Mathews)

A pack of kings and jokers: George Doonan, Tommy Trinder, Johnny Riscoe, Bud Flanagan, Albert Whelan, Ted Ray, Georgie Wood, Clarkson Rose, George Elrick, Charlie, Ben Warris and Cyril Dowler.

In his role as King Rat, with Fred Russell, Laurel and Hardy and the late Will Murray.
(T.V. Mirror)

An *entènte tres cordiale* with Maurice Chevalier.
(Matthews' News and Photo Agency)

nest Marples, former Minister of Transport having fun with Bud Flanagan,
ck Solomons and Charlie. (Matthews' News and Photo Agency)

arlie, as King Rat in 1951 with guest of honour. Charlie Chaplin, Georgie Wood,
d Fred Russell, OBE in background.

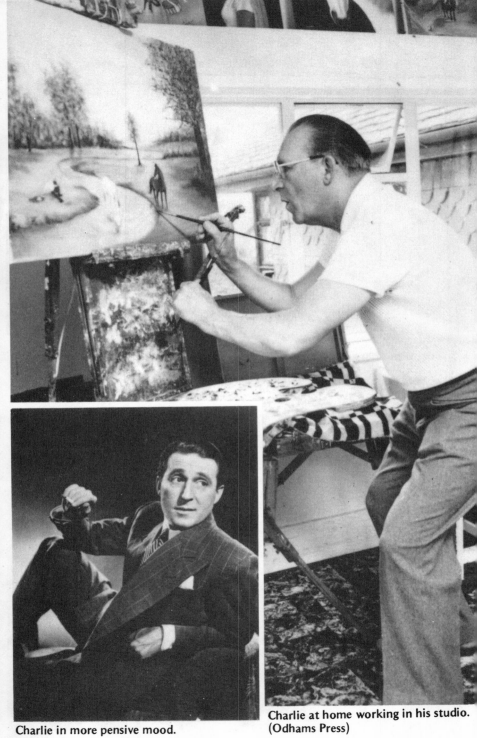

Charlie in more pensive mood.

Charlie at home working in his studio.
(Odhams Press)

things along financially and to keep herself occupied, Dorita then went for a season dancing again in Blackpool, and that was the last of her touring. Peter was born two years later on 9 September and I wasn't very popular with the nurse who attended her.

My wife always seems to do things the hard way, and whether it was from being an acrobatic dancer or not, I don't know, but she had a most difficult time with the birth. Apart from an excess of fluid, which made her whole body swell, her eyes closed so tight with the swelling that she was unable to see. She was a hundred and thirty hours in labour and from where I was stationed I sent her a telegram, when the news of a boy reached me. My telegram read:

YOU MUST BE TAKING THE BIBLE TOO
SERIOUSLY, SIX DAYS SHALT THOU LABOUR.

The nurse read this to her and when I was finally allowed to see her, I received a very chilly reception from the nurse, who must have had little sense of humour, for she thought that I was being callous; and when Peter was little more than a toddler, it was Mrs Norah Butlin who started him off on something that nearly drove us round the bend.

To occupy the little fellow one day, she gave him a pair of drum brushes to play with, and he became so intrigued he went overboard to be a drummer. Before I knew it, there were sticks, drums, bass drum, cymbals, bongos and other equipment that almost filled the large attic room. Drum rolls, beats, rhythms, breaks, para diddle – we got the lot. Practice, practice, practice. Thump, thump, thump. Many was the time I wanted to yell: "For God's sake give it a rest." But remembering my own feelings when my father said: "Tell him to make his bloody noise in his own room," I refrained.

I suddenly realised that he was very good at it and when George Firestone, the drummer at the London Palladium, said he could teach him nothing more, I knew he was right.

Then came skiffle and rock, and it had to come to our house in the form of two pals of Peter's from Tyneside, who had the most incredible appetites I have ever witnessed.

With them, Hank and Bruce, Peter formed a group called The Chesternuts and the house now, literally, reverberated with music. Then another lad came to rehearsals, a polite young man, who always used to come back down the stairs and ask: "Are you sure we're not making too much noise?"

His name was Cliff Richard.

Peter was still a pupil at Highgate school, and when he realised that Cliff could offer the boys a better chance of a good living as a group it was agreed that the two guitar players, Hank and Bruce, should go with Cliff.

They became known as The Shadows and as we all know, became one of the most popular groups in the country.

Hank has always remembered, for wherever he goes we always receive a card from him with the same message. It simply reads: HELLO FOLKS.

Peter left school and formed another group which he took to Israel, and where they were they received rave notices – in Hebrew – for bringing the "new sound" to the country. Their next stop was Germany.

But things were much tougher there, and apart from the fact that Peter had financed the whole set up – the equipment and so on – the new group were unreliable and unpunctual and so when he returned home he disbanded the group and continued writing songs for Cliff.

I have always realised how difficult it must be for children of parents "in the business". When our Peter started his schooling at Thone, which is the junior section of Taunton School, it was evident that he was being referred to as Cheerful Charlie Junior, and I asked that he should be given his own name and identification.

I realised too that he would often have things said to him such as: "You're not like the old man," or something similar, and that he would be matched against me. I had long talks with him over this in an effort to eliminate any resentment and we decided that if anyone should make any remarks about me to him, he would have a ready answer.

"Not like your old man, are you?"

"No, I'm better looking."

In this way, he was able to enjoy being my lad, and there has never been any question of resentment.

In fact, although I wasn't able to be much help to him in the "rock" world, for that was a business far removed from the entertainment I have been associated with, we have been the closest of mates, with a perfect understanding.

There have been many sons and daughters of people in show business and very few of them actually do the same things as their parents, perhaps because of the "matching".

Ted Ray is a great comedian and his two sons Andrew and Robin have both made their mark. Andrew, firstly as a child star in films such as *The Mudlark*, and later as a first-rate straight actor.

Robin, who hated his conscription, proved he could do it by becoming the best turned-out cadet of the year, and today is regularly proving his brilliance as a musician and TV panelist.

Ted and Andrew were frequent visitors to the Finchley house, as was Norman Wisdom, and the table-tennis routines were hilarious to say the least.

Will Fyffe, the famous character comedian, had a son, Will Jnr, who was an extremely fine pianist.

Another brilliant pianist too, was Ian Elrick, the son of Alice and George Elrick. Ian was on the threshold of a musical career, when he was accidentally killed by an Army motor truck when he was returning home to celebrate his twenty-first birthday. A fine son, of equally fine parents.

Young Buddy, the handsome young son of Bud and Curly Flanagan, who died so tragically from leukaemia in America, *might* have followed his Dad, but somehow I don't think he would. It was because of young Buddy's death, that the Leukaemia Wing was built at the Marsden

Hospital. Curly laid the foundation stone and the wing perpetuates the name of Bud Flanagan.

It is nice to record that some youngsters do follow the same pattern as their parents, as did Hope and Keen, the two sons of Sid and Max Harrison, the two comedians with whom I have had both the pleasure and frustration of working.

Another is Kerry Jewel, Jimmy Jewel's son, who is a comedian in his own right, and it doesn't seem so long since I saw him conduct the orchestra at a charity concert at the Victoria Palace. He was then only five years old.

Max and Harry Nesbitt were stalwarts of the variety stage who wrote and performed their own songs. Harry was probably the best snooker player in the business; he could have been a professional, yet his son, Derren Nesbitt, was neither snooker player nor comic. As we all know he made his impact on television as a dramatic actor.

One of the funniest "child" stories came from Harry Tate's son, Ronnie. He recalls that when he was a babe in arms, his mother travelled with him in the back seat of the car, and Harry, who was famous for his "motoring" sketch, did the driving, and sitting up front by the side of him, was the man he employed as his "feed". It seems that Harry and his "feed" were constantly having violent arguments. Harry would sack him every other day, and then take him on again.

On this particular occasion, one Sunday in the car, the usual heated argument started and got out of hand, culminating with the "feed" saying that he would rather get out and walk. Harry pulled up the car, opened the door, and told him to do just that. Harry then drove on, leaving the poor devil to paddle along behind.

At some distance ahead, however, a very large bumble bee flew in the rear window and then up and under Mrs. Tate's long, voluminous skirts, whereupon it stung her high up on her thigh.

She began to scream blue murder and Harry said:

"Well there's only one thing to do." So saying, he flung her skirts up and began to attempt to suck the offending "sting" out.

After a few moments of this the old "feed" had drawn level with the car and as he passed, still in high dudgeon, he looked in the car, saw Harry and shouted in the window: ". . . and that's rather naughty. In front of the kid, you ought to be more discreet."

Contentment can be enjoyed alone,
but real happiness is best when shared.

CHAPTER SIX

Always give yourself an opportunity to think
and thinking of others . . .
there's always an opportunity to give.

I MENTIONED earlier about the Variety profession's brother-
hood, The Grand Order of Water Rats. This great or-
ganisation was first formed in the late 1800s when Dan
Leno, Harry Freeman, Wal Pink, Cinquevalli, Little Titch,
Chirgwin and other great names, were topping the Music
Halls.

The name of the organization came out of an incident
when several of them got together and bought a little pony,
which was originally known as the "Magpie". They hitched
it to a buggy and went to the races at Epsom.

On the way, however, the heavens opened, it poured with
rain, and they were all soaked to the skin. The little animal

looked so bedraggled that a bus driver opened his window and shouted: "What have you got there? It looks like a bloody water rat."

After the laughter subsided they began to think a little deeper on the subject, the result was The Grand Order of Water Rats.

There was a good deal of serious thought attached to this name for the idea was to name themselves after the lowliest of animals, and try to uplift it to the highest in their ideals and aims.

Take the word "rats" backwards, and you have the word "star" and each member, regardless of his fame, should endeavour to be a star in the firmament of conviviality, good fellowship and charity.

It is an order with its own charter, and has its many secrets, but from the day the charter was granted to the present, the members have tried to emulate those men before them, and to help, not only their own, but every other deserving charity.

I think it might be fair to say that performers, whether they be members of the Grand Order of Water Rats or not, must be among the most charitable of all people, for they are always being asked to give their services to some function or other and I don't know many who haven't willingly done so.

A great number of the GOWR members are also members of the VGS (The Vaudeville Golfing Society).

This is probably one of the most exclusive golfing societies in the world. Their Annual Stag Night, at the Park Lane Hotel, is a sell out every year, probably because it is just about the sauciest night anyone could wish to attend. It's the greatest of fun, and being performers quite a lot of it is very clever. The after-dinner speeches have to be heard to be believed and are an entertainment out of this world.

I have spoken myself many times, and I can remember being the eighth speaker on one occasion, following such performers as Ted Ray, Tommy Trinder, Bob Pearson (of Bob and Alf Pearson), Leslie Sarony, Dickie Henderson, Jimmy Wheeler and Cardew Robinson, to mention but a few. One of the guests of honour was a medical man, Arthur Dixon Wright, one of the finest after-dinner speakers I have met.

The whole evening at the Stag Night is one of surprises, and although people have got to know this, we still manage to spring surprises on them.

Some years ago the speakers had been chosen and they all prepared their speeches carefully, and it wasn't until they sat down and saw the menu card with the toast list, they realised that the guest of honour was from Australia, the Bishop of Perth.

Quite a number were panic stricken, saying that they were now lumbered, their speech was far too blue, and what a ridiculous thing to invite *him* to the do.

Hurriedly they rewrote their notes and their dinner was spoiled I'm sure with worrying about how far they should go. They all managed their speeches and toned them down accordingly, so as not to offend the celebrated clerical guest of honour.

When the old Bishop got up to speak, he started with something like:

"Mister Chairman and gentlemen, I can't tell you how much I have enjoyed myself thus far, and I must say that you have dispelled the earlier remarks I heard when they told me that you were a dirty lot of bastards . . ."

It was not long before the audience realised that they had been hoaxed. It was an actor, employed specially for the purpose. The speakers made up for it later in the cabaret, so nothing was wasted.

Together with the Committee, we secretly arranged things and I pulled this kind of hoax on them on quite a few occasions.

The first time was when Christine Jorgensen hit the headlines after her sex-change operation.

I was listed at the Annual Ball as Christine Jorgensen, who would reply for the ladies. For three weeks prior to the event I started to practise walking in high-heeled shoes. I grew my finger nails long and had them shaped, and on the day of the event, I spent several hours shaving all the hair off my chest and under arms. I had the closest shave ever and then took great pains to put on a good make up and had a special wig. I also bought a gown that fitted me like a glove and after much laborious work I had transformed myself into a "passable woman".

It was decided that I should go separately from my wife, she would be escorted by friends, and I would take a taxi to Richard Afton's home, and he would escort me, together with Gill his wife.

When I paid the taxi man, I felt that I might get away with it, when he called out: "Goodnight Miss," to me.

As I entered Dickie's home he stood with his mouth open and couldn't believe it, and Gill was so fascinated she kept walking round me staring hard and falling about laughing. We let her get it out of her system as we wanted it all to be quite serious when we got there.

Richard Afton himself can be quite a sphinx so he was perfect. He walked into the Grosvenor House Hotel with us both, one on each arm and immediately my make-up was put to the test.

Alice Elrick was standing in the hall, right in our path. She said hello to Dickie and Gill as we passed, and nodded to me as if I were a total stranger. The first hurdle was over. Next, I was secluded away until the MC shouted: "Dinner is served," and I was hustled in with the throng.

I sat at a table for eight and my wife sat at a different table. The men each side of me were primed to keep talking to me so that all I needed to do was nod. They lit my cigarettes for me and I rolled my long silk mittens back, I daren't take them off, for they hid the tattoo I have on one wrist.

All was going well, until someone from behind a menu

was heard to whisper: "Who is the old bag with Dickie Afton?"

I was rewarded in one way for Reg Ellsmore was one side of me giving me so much attention, that his wife got a little cross with him for doing so. Only five people knew it was me, and yet one little waitress came and whispered in my ear: "Excuse me, but have I guessed something?" A hurried whisper back to her and all was well.

When I was announced to reply for the ladies, I had a rousing reception and the women craned their necks to get a better view. Two sentences from me and I exploded the myth, and I have never heard such a roar from an audience. I had a ball for the next twenty minutes and began to get some pleasure following what had been two hours of frustration, and, at times, embarrassment.

The next occasion was a few years later when I went masquerading as Doctor Kinsey, and on that occasion I had to reply to Doctor Edith Summerskill. I remember saying on that occasion that, although a doctor, I doubted that I could tell her anything about "labour pains".

On the occassion of the visit to this country of the two Saudi Arabian princes, they made a tremendous impact and had lots of press publicity, for they looked so much alike, and were very striking in their National costume.

The VGS Ball was due at this time. An enormous crowd attended the function and when the Master of Ceremonies announced that we had been honoured by a visit from their Royal Highnesses, they appeared on the balcony at the top of the staircase and were rapturously received. Their national anthem was played by the band, and the audience below them all stood in homage and respect.

After the anthem, the two princes walked erect and with grace down the long stairway, and at about eight steps from the bottom the band broke into a musical introduction. It was perfectly timed, for as they stepped on to the floor they went into a simultaneous tap routine that lifted the roof. They were, of course, two professional dancers.

In my years as King Rat I had three celebrated guests at different functions: Charlie Chaplin, Maurice Chevalier, and Jimmy "Schnozzle" Durante. I couldn't have had three greater stars or three nicer people.

It was in 1952. I was the youngest King Rat since Dan Leno. Sitting on my right at a dinner in his honour, was the great Charlie Chaplin, himself a Water Rat. It was many years since he had started his show-business career, although I doubt if he'll ever forget *Mumming Birds* (one of his earliest shows) or the famous Casey's Court, belonging to Will Murray, who employed Charlie and later sacked him.

During the course of the evening, I was able to tell him of how, as a young boy, I used to be taken to see his films, but what he didn't know at the time, was that Will Murray himself, then over eighty, was a member of the vast audience. He was, however, far removed from the top table.

I remember during my speech, as an aside, asking Charlie if he would like to meet his old boss. He politely smiled at me and nodded, whereupon I called for Will to come to the top table.

It took the old fellow some time to get there and during this Charlie smiled, thinking it was a gag of some sort. However, as Will Murray got nearer to the top table Charlie saw it was him and in disbelief he said in a hushed voice: "Guv'nor!"

Immediately I quipped: "Why not ask him for a rise?"

Quick as a flash he retorted: "I can't. He sacked me!"

By the time the laughter filled the great hall the two men had clasped hands and both had tears in their eyes. Although at the time I was honoured with the exalted position of King Rat, I can honestly say the sight of these two men made me feel quite humble.

'Schnozzle' Durante, that lovable American comedian and character, was a different man completely. He was vaudeville. Loud, rumbustious, an extrovert in the truest sense. I loved this man from our first meeting.

It had been arranged that he would be the guest of honour, but, that as King Rat, I would go to the Palladium and formally ask him to attend the banquet.

To give a clear picture of what actually happened I have to explain that number one dressing room, is really two rooms, connected by a door. On entering you walk through one room and into a smaller room, which is usually the one used for dressing in, and the larger room for entertaining guests.

Opposite the door in the larger room is a divan, several small chairs, a drinks trolley. The whole room thing is rather plush.

When Bert, the stage door keeper, went in to announce that King Rat, Charlie Chester had arrived, I heard a voice bellow: "Come in King Charlie!"

I went through the large room and noticed a beautiful young girl sitting alone on the divan. I nodded politely to her as I went through and entered the smaller room, where Jimmy was having a rub down by his faithful friend and partner, Jackson.

The loud voice and "King Charlie" routine had me smiling from the word go. We soon got talking about vaudeville and burlesque in America and the subject finally came around to bootleggers and prohibition. I can't remember the exact conversation but I do know that it was the funniest I have ever been engaged in.

He slowly got dressed and then said: "Where are you gonna take me to eat? I want some Jewish cookin'."

I had a quick think and remembering that there was a good Jewish restuarant close to Piccadilly, I told him we would go to Lex Garage.

"A garage . . . to *eat*? I've heard of a filling station, but that's ridiculous," he said, flinging his arms out in the usual way.

"It's OK," I replied. "There's a restaurant above the garage."

"OK King Charlie! Lead the way." Every gesture, every intonation, was exactly the same as delivered on the screen.

He, Jackson and I, then came out from the small room into the larger room and as we entered he saw the girl, who couldn't have been much more than about seventeen or eighteen, sitting on the divan. I had completely forgotten about her.

"Come on honey," he shouted to her. Without more ado, she joined us as we trooped out. As we left the building Schnozzle pulled me to one side and whispered, if whispered is the word, "King Charlie . . . I wanna sit next to the goil!" There seemed a pleading in his voice. "It's your prerogative," I replied.

Jackson and I occupied the bucket seats and he reclined with the young lady, and started to make a fuss of her. He had his hand on her knee, then around her waist; he kissed her on the cheek and she acquiesced. Jackson and I made conversation between ourselves and politely ignored them.

When we arrived at the restaurant, Jimmy pulled me aside again and repeated as before: "I wanna sit next to da goil!"

"Well of course."

Up to this she had said nothing. Her knees and thighs had been well patted, and she had been kissed and cuddled, but from her – not a word.

We sat the young lady down and left the seat next to her for Jimmy. Jackson and I sat facing them. Then Jimmy announced that he wanted to phone his mother in Italy. This put the place in an uproar, for into the old-fashioned phone hanging on the wall, he bellowed: "Gimme Italy. I wanna talk to mah mudder!" Truth to tell he could almost have done so without the use of the phone. When he finally got through, he was shouting: "Ma . . . ahm havin' dinner wid King Charlie!" It was hilarious while it lasted.

Then he returned to the table and ordered his food. During the time it took to bring it, the girl's knees and legs had further attention from this exuberant man, and she

142

reaped a few more kisses and squeezes, and still she said nothing. She just smiled.

When it was time to go back to the Palladium, we went through the routine again. "I wanna sit next to the goil."

In the taxi the same again, the knees, the legs, the squeezes, the pats, the kisses, and there was Jackson and I pretending it wasn't happening.

When we finally arrived back, we all got out of the taxi and for the first time I heard the young lady speak.

She said: "Well, I think I'd better be going now!"

"OK honey," he said, and kissed her again, and she tripped away.

Immediately she had gone Schnozzle looked at me with those gimlet eyes, and with his head on one side in typical fashion he said to me: "Who was da goil?"

I was flabbergasted.

"I don't know," I answered. "I thought she was with you!"

"Dat's funny," he said. "Ah t'ought she wuz wid you!"

Somewhere there's a young lady who had a hilarious lunch, was kissed, caressed and squeezed by the great little man, and to this day, neither I nor Jimmy knows her name.

I suppose that Schnozzle Durante could be classed as one of the great 'characters' of American vaudeville and I think it would be fair to say that "Monsewer" Eddie Gray was one of the last of the great comedy "characters" of variety in this country.

Eddie was probably one of the most cruel of all the jokers – an absolute terror. I called to see him one day at the Victoria Palace. It was in the heat of a very hot summer and he was sitting in his dressing room with the door open. He must have heard me coming because he picked up the phone and pretended to be in conversation with his book-maker.

He looked up as I entered and said: "Hello," then went on

talking, saying that six thousand was too much to lose in any one week.

I knew it was a "take on" so I told him not to waste his time. He put the phone down and said: "Horses!" and then let out a string of invectives that outclassed anything I had heard in the army. Just as he did this, however, a woman passed the door, and he noticed her.

He was sitting there in just his socks and shoes and with his comedy moustache on, apart from this he was stark naked. When he heard the door further up the passage re-open a little later, he sprang up and went to the door in time to confront the woman as she returned down the passage to go out.

The poor woman didn't know which way to look, she was so embarrassed at his complete nudity.

"Madame," he said. "I've got to apologise to you."

"No, no . . . it's quite all right Mister Gray," she stuttered, looking anywhere but at him.

"No, no, I insist," he went on, barring her pathway. "You see when you went past my door I was entertaining my friend in there, and I used some awful language, and you must have heard me."

"It's quite all right Mister Gray, really!" The poor woman was going all the colours of the rainbow.

"It was very wrong of me and I'm ashamed of myself, because it's not a nice thing to do in front of a lady is it?"

"Mister Gray, really . . . I didn't hear . . ." She wanted to get away from him.

"So you will accept my apology then?"

"Yes, yes, of course."

"Oh thank you. That makes me feel much better, you're very kind, and I feel the least I can do is see you to the stage door."

He took her by the arm, naked as he was, and went to escort her. She shrank away in horror lest anyone should see them together.

She was fighting a losing battle. He did escort her right to the stage door, and she hurried away faster than I have seen anyone go, either before or since.

One of Eddie's favourite tricks, especially when working with the Gang, was to remove his underpants and just keep his shirt on, and then walk into the other boys' room, where they might have a guest – all the better if it were a woman. He would pretend to be searching the floor for something, he would turn his back on the visitor and then bend forward, revealing his backside and back up to them saying: "Have you seen a collar stud?" With someone's derriere in your face it's not easy to carry on a normal conversation.

When Arthur Askey had a series on radio called *Can I Come In*, he would go by BBC car with two guests, to the home of a particular family. The engineers preceded us and would have everything ready for us when we arrived. It was a comedy chat and music show.

On the occasion when Eddie Gray and I were guests, we had to go to a family in Petersfield. Eddie, Arthur, the producer and I were in the back of the car, and after travelling for some time, the driver admitted he was lost.

After travelling for miles down leafy lanes and seeing no one who might be able to give us directions we suddenly saw an old gentleman in the distance.

"There's someone we can ask," the producer said with relief. The driver accelerated and then pulled up with a squeal of brakes. Eddie flashed out and suddenly confronted the poor soul, shook him like a rat and shouted: "Where in heaven's name have you been. We shan't wait for you again!"

Thereupon he jumped back in the car and the driver sped on.

"Which way sir?" he asked.

"I don't know," said Eddie. "The poor old man never even answered me."

Jimmy Nervo, knowing that Eddie didn't mind walking in

145

naked if they had guests, went to his room one day and said:
"Ed, we've got a young lady visitor in our room, come in
with nothing on in a minute. You know, the old gag!"

"OK." Eddie agreed.

A few minutes later, he walked into their room, dressed
like a modern day streaker and as he went in, suddenly the
door slammed shut behind him. The young lady, happened
to be Florence Desmond, the famous impressionist, and she
said: "You filthy beast!" What she did to teach him a lesson
with a rolled up newspaper, I'm sure he never forgot.

The women have often proved themselves to be just as
good as the men at playing tricks.

Thora Hird is one such woman. Apart from being a
wonderful actress, she knows her comedy as only the
specialist can. One thing she could do, better than anyone
I know, was cry. She can make tears roll down her cheeks
at will.

It was with this ploy that she gave me an amusing and
embarrassing few moment at the Blue Parrot, in Blackpool.
This was a restaurant where the pros went to eat after
their shows and I happened to be all alone, sitting at a
table there. The holiday makers would often stand outside
to see who would be coming, and the place was usually full
of holiday people anyway.

I lowered my eyes and began to eat my food, knowing that
I was being watched, when suddenly someone stopped at
my table and started to rant at me.

"Oh so there you are, stuffing yourself. Oh yes, it's all
right for you, don't you ever think of the five kids you ran
away and left me with! You rotter!"

I went cold for a second. Every eye in the restaurant was
on me, and all went quiet, waiting for the balloon that they
thought must go up. The management looked apprehensive,
and there was this woman, sobbing her heart out, raving at
me about the kids with no food, and there was I stuffing
myself.

Suddenly she took her hand away from her face and I could see that it was Thora Hird.

"Sit down you silly bitch," I said, and we fell about laughing.

"I'll get my own back on you for that little performance," I promised.

We had a most enjoyable meal, her husband joined us and we talked of sundry things and finally we talked about material.

I told her that I had written a little monologue about a clown and that it was terribly sad.

She wanted me to tell it to her, which I did, and before I had finished, she was weeping again. This time sensitive tears. She was very moved indeed.

"I would love to have a little party piece like that," she said. "You know, something I can suddenly start to say at a party, and for the people listening not to know that it was an actual piece of material, and by the time they realised it, I would be well into it."

"I know the kind of thing you mean," I replied. "I tell you what Thora, I'll write one specially for you."

"Would you really love," she said.

"Sure I will, I'll bring it to you later this week."

I wrote a devastating piece of heart rendery about a little boy who saved up all his pennies to buy his mother a huge bouquet of flowers that the florist had wrapped in cellophane in the window. He kept going with more pennies and wanted to know if he was near the target. The days went by and finally he picked up the flowers from the shop and ran home with the present for his mother. As he drew alongside the house, he saw his mother on the opposite side of the road, and called to her in excitement: "Happy birthday," and dashed across the road, whereupon he was knocked down and killed. The flowers meant for his Mum becoming the flowers on his grave.

It was an awful piece of slush really.

I took it to the theatre where Thora was performing, and I timed it so that she was almost ready to go on. I began to read it to her, and knowing that I had written it for her, she was too polite to say: "Not now."

She listened to it as she made her way to the corner ready to go on, and by the time I had finished it, she was sobbing her heart out, and her mascara had run all down her face. I suddenly said: "You're on Thora."

"You swine!" was all she could say.

"I told you I'd get my own back," I said.

What a character Thora is; what a woman and what an artiste.

In the Vaudeville Golfing Society there have been several very good golfers, Jerry Desmonde and Sid Field were both very short handicap men, as was Donald Peers. And Jewel and Warriss may have been funny men on stage, but they were very serious about their golf.

I have never been very good at it and part of my gamesmanship is to open up with a funny gag that makes my opponent laugh and then keep repeating the tag line as we go round.

I have never really wanted to be a short handicap player because the game gets far too serious.

There used to be a story about Henry Cotton, who was well known as a man whose temper was not always as sweet as it might have been.

The story goes that he was putting on the links at Eastbourne and was taking his time over one particularly long putt, when suddenly, he threw down the club and exclaimed with exasperation: "How the hell can you concentrate with all this bloody traffic in the channel!?"

On one occasion my agent Charles Tucker was sitting with me in the audience at Blackpool. We were guests at the show and Joseph Locke was top of the bill. In those days he was the doyen of the North. He mentioned that I was in the audience and I was given the customary "big hand". He then

148

announced that the man sitting next to me was the world famous golfer Bobby Locke.

After the show, immediately the lights went up, we were both surrounded by autograph hunters who wanted "Mr Locke" and me to sign.

Charlie Tucker had no option but to sign. After a few minutes I noticed what he was doing and I had to hiss in his ear: "If you're going to sign as Bobby Locke, for God's sake spell it with an 'E'."

Frederick Ferrari was very keen as a golfer and once, when we played at Brighton, we had caddies. Fred had a very young schoolboy golf addict, a little Jewish boy, who had caddied the previous week for Bobby Locke. Every time Fred teed up for a drive, his caddie would say: "Bobby Locke took a three iron from here and he was on."

Just before taking his shot, Fred found this very off putting. Every shot he squared up for, he was told just what Bobby Locke did, and in the end Fred was seething. At the eighteenth tee, he squared up to the short green and up piped the voice: "Bobby Locke took a seven iron here and was six inches from the pin!" Fred stopped. He glared at the kid and said sweetly: "Can Bobby Locke sing?"

The kid replied. "I don't think so!"

Fred almost screamed at him. "Well that's the bloody difference!"

I have heard many funny expressions on the course, but the one that made me smile most was Arthur Haynes, when playing at Sudbury.

As you tee off from the second there are two fairways, separated by a long line of bushes only. Arthur hit a banana slice and the ball went straight over to the other fairway on the right. When he arrived at the spot the ball had sunk below the surface of the ground into a rut that had been made by someone taking an enormous divot in wet weather.

I watched him from behind the bushes to see if he would pick the ball out.

He peered down at the ball below the surface of the ground, then scratched his head and I heard him mumble to himself: "I don't know whether to take a four iron or a benzedrine tablet!"

I think perhaps the strangest and funniest match I ever witnessed was in Blackpool, and this occurred after the Annual Ball.

Jimmy Edwards and Jimmy Wheeler had been imbibing, which they could do more handsomely and professionally than any other two I know. They were both high as kites when a game of golf was suggested. To see these two men, pickled, playing golf by moonlight in full evening dress, was hilarious.

Every season, of course, the VGS played St Annes Old Links, and after the match there is an alfresco concert and high jinks in general.

One year, I was standing there when a Dutch auction was suggested, and Ben Warriss was the auctioneer. He spotted me and suggested that I was wearing a beautiful tie which would be very good for auction, so they ripped it off and flogged it. After this I reached in my pocket for a cigarette and before I knew it my gold cigarette case went, plus my lighter. I was lucky to escape with my trousers intact.

I have always been a twenty-four handicap man, and when I first took up the game I was inveigled into a match where I was partnered with a pro, Keith Hargreaves, the Lancashire champion. Nothing daunted, however, he was coaching me around and telling me what to do.

I remember on one short hole, there was a pond in front of us behind which was a group of trees, and directly behind these, the green. The pond was naturally a magnet for balls from players like me and Keith said: "Forget the pond and trees, just take the club, slow back, head down, follow through and have all the confidence in the world."

I did exactly as he told me and by freak of chance the ball sailed straight over the pond, then over the trees and on to the green, rolling to within three inches of the pin. I have never again made a shot as good. The first three scores eight, two, and ten.

Being a long handicap player can sometimes be an embarrassment, for one is liable to pull one or two out of the bag by sheer chance. Playing on another occasion against Bill Shanklin, the golf pro from Potters Bar, he asked me before starting what my handicap was. His caddie and he were quite understanding when I told them twenty-four. I teed up at the first and with a prayer swung at the ball. It turned out to be one of those rare occasions when it all happened right. A blinder of a shot, long, straight, a marvellous crack from the golf club which tells you you've hit a good one.

I heard the caddie whisper to Bill: "Where did he get his handicap, in the desert?"

As well as golf, I also took up archery, and for a while I was with the London Archers. I was more proficient with the bow and arrow than with the golf club.

In America they play archery golf, which is most interesting, for a reasonable archer can play a scratch golfer and give him a good game. The rules make this possible, for the archer is only allowed to use one bow. He can't for instance use a strong heavy bow to get distance, and then a lighter bow for the exactness of putting. He must use the same bow and must, at each shot, do a full draw. You are not allowed to tweak the arrow up and over, so to speak.

If, for example, you were twenty yards from the hole, and the green was high up on a kind of plateau, which many of them are, you must either do a full draw high into the air, attempting to get your arrow on the green, or aim, for a high point and then another arrow from there to putt out.

The putting, in the archer's case, is done into a wire ring the same size as the hole, situated level with the actual hole. If, during play, the archer's arrow goes into a bunker, he forfeits two shots, and if the arrow goes to within a bow's length of a bunker, he forfeits one shot. This levels things up

151

with a scratch player, for they have the benefit of the ball rolling, whereas once an arrow hits the ground, the next shot is taken from behind that arrow.

I challenged Bill Shanklin at Butlins Holiday Camp in Clacton, to an archery golf match. It was part of a big charity tournament.

What a match it was! The crowd we pulled was fantastic and I was two up on him at the turn. But what a player he is; he not only beat me three and one, but to do that he broke the course record, returning a gross sixty-two off a seventy-three bogey and on his card were three eagles and five birdies.

Ted Ray put me off my game once at Finchley, and I wasn't even playing with him. I happened to be among the four following him and he must have known this, because when we arrived at one tee, there was a ball already teed up waiting for me and by the side of it lay a dead mouse with a note tied to its tail. It simply read: "Charlie, I died waiting for you," and it was signed "Georgie Wood." I played terrible golf after that, but I grinned like a Cheshire cat all the way round.

Both the VGS and the Grand Order of Water Rats have afforded me some of the greatest happiness I have known and in the case of the latter it seems to have turned full circle, for whereas the Order was founded and named after the little pony taking stars to Epsom Races, we now have our own racehorse called The Water Rat.

There is a syndicate of ten, including Billy Butlin, Danny La Rue, Frankie Vaughan, myself and several others, who purchased the filly from the trainer Doug Marks when she was called Mame.

We changed her name to The Water Rat. She made excellent showing and had great gameness; in one race she was knocked to her knees at the start but picked herself up and came third. She won about five races and was placed in many others.

She has now been a mother twice. Once by Reliance, from

which we had a lovely young filly, and then by Shiny Tenth, producing the bonniest colt, in which we have great hopes.

To benefit from life, surely
we must share life's benefits.

CHAPTER SEVEN

*Surely the finest cause to fight for is the one to
eliminate the cause for fighting.*

WE used to have a far flung Empire, but let's face it, we
couldn't have flung it much farther. Nevertheless, entertaining the troops in all the outposts has given me the opportunity of visiting places which I would never have gone to
in the normal way of things.

From Al Adem to Tripoli, and several times up and down
the Persian Gulf. From Aden to Bahrein, including places
like Solala, Mazira, Shahjah and Dubai. Some of the
larger places are quite comfortable to work in, apart from
the extreme heat. The Astra at Bahrein, and the theatre at
Steamer Point in Aden, are both open-air theatres which
afford all the facilities and atmosphere that one could
hope for. Yet there's nothing quite so rewarding as
entertaining a small handful of men, stuck out in the desert,

155

who probably haven't seen a strange face for some time.

This vast expanse of rolling waste has witnessed so many phases of man's temperament, the blazing guns of battle, shattered tanks and bodies, the raucous laughter of the troops being entertained and the contrasting sounds of screaming shells, to the plaintive playing of an old accordion.

The fact that the desert is so undulating, means that from the road tracks there could be a group of men being entertained quite close at hand, and yet completely out of sight to anyone driving past.

One of the code of ethics in the desert is in the cause of hygiene and to this end they would sink petrol tins at intervals along the track, for the purpose of urinating. It was a practice strictly observed.

When the Americans first arrived on the scene in the desert one particular GI was hurrying along in his jeep in the moonlight, and what he didn't know was that there was a group of men being entertained just off the roadway behind a sand dune. One of the performers, in full evening dress and top hat, had wandered across to the track to urinate in the proper place. As he calmly stood there, using the bucket, so elegantly dressed, the American jeep suddenly screamed to a halt and all the American could say was: "Jesus Christ! I don't believe it . . ." and drove on. I often wonder if that American still believes the evidence of his own eyes.

It seemed so unreal to me on my first visit to the Middle East, especially in these days of jet air travel, to be in the metropolis one moment, and the next, watching a camel train slowly plodding its way across the desert on the horizon. It was fascinating to see the women still covering their faces with their yashmaks. In that part of the globe the women certainly do seem to be second-class citizens. As visitors to their country we had to be careful and to observe their customs and respect them.

With my party I had a double act who had only been married a short while, and they couldn't resist walking hand-in-hand along the street, and for doing so they had stones thrown at them, for it isn't considered right to walk by the side of your spouse, let alone stroll hand-in-hand.

The first time I played at Aden, I was fascinated to see goats wearing brassieres. At least the udders and teats were covered by some hessian material, so that the young kids were unable to suckle. I assume that the milk was a commodity reserved for human consumption. Anyway, reference to the goats and their bras afforded me quite a lot of laughs from the stage.

To carry out our tour of entertainment up and down the Gulf, the Army provided us with a plane, and an Air Force pilot and sergeant. We performed at one place close to the Yemeni border, in the heat of the midday sun with the lads all sitting on the ground, and after the show we had a look around. There was some sort of market going on, which we wandered into. At first they were intrigued with us, especially at the modern attire of our females, but as we wandered around, buying a few odd bits of rubbish, we noticed that the atmosphere was becoming quite hostile.

There was nothing to tell us that we had gone over the Yemeni border, and to escape without too much fuss – realising that they liked our money more than us – we loaded ourselves up with stuff and explained that we would be back to spend a lot more, after we had taken what we had already purchased home.

It was the thoughts of us returning to spend a lot more, that got us out without an "incident".

The thing which fascinated me most about these Yemeni "warriors" – if that is the right word for them – was the fact that they all carried cumbersome long-barrelled, old-fashioned rifles, and around their bodies they were swathed in bandoliers and belts of ammunition. The amusing part for me, was that the rifle was such a relic, none of the ammunition would have fitted it anyway. It just seemed to be a status symbol to walk about looking like an arsenal.

We were once housed in an old fort in the desert, miles

away from civilisation. It was originally used by the old French Foreign Legion, and it certainly made me realise what a spartan existence it must have been, when the Foreign Legion was the place to where the "outcasts of society" migrated.

The sheiks of the various areas and territories, are, of course, the king rulers and their word is law. Some of them are quite vain, they won't even allow British Army officers, driving staff cars, to overtake them when driving their limousines.

The Arab laws are harsh and indeed primitive, an habitual thief can get his hand chopped off. We heard of a man who had committed an offence for which he was strapped to the oil pipe line and flogged publicly.

To an ordinary observer like me, passing through, it does seem that the gulf between affluence and poverty is so vast there. In fact there seems to be no middle class, it's either the big cars and diamond rings, or the beggar calling for Baksheesh.

I was saddened to see the sight of so many twisted cripples hobbling along. We may grumble about our social services but to see "how the other half" lives brings a measure of comfort.

The question of one particular sheik's vanity arose at a place we visited, which was merely a small pocket of soldiers out in the desert, and for us to put on their show for them they had worked all day filling bags with sand and making a stage. These they covered with flat boards, made a sort of proscenium arch and fixed up some gaudy drapes. Where they managed to find all the material I just don't know, but they even had paint to daub the word Palladium over the front.

They next brought all the jeeps and vehicles to face the stage and backed them away, leaving a space for the lads to sit on the sand, and then switched on all the headlights. This was our stage lighting.

When it comes to improvisation, there's no one better

than the troops and improvisation was the thing I had to do when the officer told me we mustn't finish the show with *God Save The Queen*.

When I asked why, the officers explained that the sheik was coming to the show, and that he would take it as a personal slight if we sang the anthem. I was naturally a little incensed about this. I had come to entertain British Forces and I didn't like the idea of a sheik telling us what we could or could not do.

But we had our instructions. *God Save The Queen* was to be deleted. At the end of the performance, however, I did my finale piece with the whole company on the stage, and then I signalled to the drummer who began to play the usual drum roll which normally preceded the anthem. I saw the officer in the front blanch, and the Sheik, resplendent in his robes, looked a little apprehensive.

Suddenly I banged one foot against the other to attention in good old military style, and started to sing *Should Auld Acquaintance Be Forgot* just as though it was the National Anthem and the entire audience of lads got up, stood to attention, and sang it with me with such reverence it *could* have been the National Anthem.

It was quite a moving moment, and although I had kept to instructions, I felt that British pride had been vindicated.

It always struck me as amazing, how a rough, tough, soldier can be so gentle and soft-hearted at times. In most areas it's possible to pick up a pet such as a dog, or something of that nature, but the prettiest I ever saw was in a desert outpost, where, strolling around the officers mess, as tame as a kitten, was Bambi, a spindly legged young fawn. It was delightful, and so affectionate. Unfortunately, on our return visit, they told us that it had eaten some rat poison and had died.

Wherever we went we were always offered to be taken to the places of interest and at Bahrein I went to a place called Oil Drum Village, and that's exactly what it was. A complete village, ingeniously built from oil drums.

Some of these people became intimate friends and even asked us to go to prayers with them. Sharing with them, if only for a short while, their way of life, makes you come away feeling a little grateful that you belong to the Western world.

The heat of the desert in the day time is uncomfortable and tiring, and to dress up and add greasepaint, is even worse. After two minutes on stage I was a wringing ball of perspiration, shirt and suit stuck to me, but somehow, when those boys started to laugh, and it got louder and louder, it all seemed worth it.

Having played up and down the Gulf, it was a very good starting point to get used to the heat. A lot further east though, it was hotter still. The hottest place I remember was Kuala Lumpur. At one time it was close to 130 in the shade. I have never known it so hot.

We did an allotted number of performances at various places in that area and then were taken to what they called a "Change of Air Station". This was a full day's journey by jeep, up through mountainous jungle, to the Cameroons. It was like going back a thousand years, for on this journey I saw pygmies, stark naked, standing unabashed, carrying their deadly blow pipes. To think that we had flown half way across the world in a matter of hours and here I was, confronted by primitive man, who had advanced so little was, to me, fascinating.

I enjoyed Singapore immensely, but was even more impressed with Nairobi. We were lucky there. They gave us two days leave and we were able to go through the Safari Game Reserve, and to be so close to the wild animals in their natural habitat was a joy that I shall always remember.

Then it was back to work and we went on to Lake Naivasha, to play to the lads in the outlying parts. We were housed at a place with chalets which stood by the side of the lake and managed by a very striking and competent woman.

Unfortunately at the time, they were still experiencing Mau Mau problems and the woman told us to lock our doors at night. She explained that her house boy, who had been faithful to her for seven years, had just taken off with a chopper after trying to decapitate her.

The fact that she had been a police woman in Liverpool saved her life.

I made doubly sure my door was locked at night, by jamming a chair under the handle.

At that time there seemed to be a permanent state of unrest, for the Kikuyu tribe would invade Masai territory and steal their wives and animals, and then the Masai would take reprisals.

The Masai warriors are a tall breed of man and very proud. Although they were still quite primitive, they were cunning enough to know that if they changed into Western attire at nights they could purchase whisky. This they did, and one night when I was walking alone through the shopping area, I noticed a giant of a man padding along behind me. I slowed up, and in an effort to let him pass me, I pretended to tie a shoelace. He drew alongside and stopped. It was a Masai warrior and he was drunk.

He looked at me balefully and towered above me. I straightened up then, ready to bolt at a moment's notice, I tried to humour him.

"You must be Masai," I said. "You big, strong . . ." I went on in admiring tones with accompanying gestures.

He nodded and agreed. "Me Masai."

I squeezed the top of his arm. "You . . . Big muscle . . . Much strong." I let him know that I was impressed and his baleful glare disappeared. By the time we said goodbye, he wanted to give me all his money. For me, it was an interesting encounter, and a test of diplomacy and psychology.

During the Korean war I went to entertain the troops and we had quite an eventful journey. We had a little oil trouble and had to touch down in Rome, where because of the delay, we were offered a tour of the city. It was an added bonus for us and all went well until we reached Bangkok, in Thailand. Here we had to change a port engine. Once again we sampled the delights of another beautiful, but strange place. Then we left for Hong Kong – a paradise; I loved the way Eastern and Western styles blended. I saw limousines outside the Peninsular Hotel at Kowloon, side by side with rickshaws. The ferry that went from Kowloon to Hong Kong was gaily lit with coloured lights, and the Chinese girls looked so lovely in their close fitting cheongsams. From what I saw of the slit skirts it seemed that the higher up the social scale, the higher the slit in the skirt, so I saw quite a lot of the "best people".

After playing to the men out there in the territories we went on to Tokyo. We arrived at midnight, in the middle of a hurricane and broke a wheel when we landed. The pilot, however, was cool, calm and very competent. He took off again as the wheels touched the ground and made a second landing on the short runway.

A brief stay at Ebisu Camp and we were on our way again. This first stay was long enough for me to appreciate just how much the Japanese and Chinese love laundering. A Japanese girl called Haneda, was detailed to look after me and in the morning, when I got up to shave, I removed the top part of my pyjamas and laid it on the bed. While I was shaving Haneda scuttled in like a rabbit, whipped the pymaja top off the bed and hurried out again. Before I had finished my shave, it was back, washed, ironed and neatly folded, and she waited for the bottom half!

On this brief stay, we were also feted by the British dignitaries serving there, and in the grounds of the palace we were to be regaled with a song in English, that the little Geisha girls had learned – phonetically, because none of them understood English. They had been taught by the soldiers.

They were all very nervous and shy, and to sing to us they asked if they could be allowed to form a circle facing each other. Suddenly their piping voices began. The soldiers who taught them deserve six month's jail, because they sang the

162

filthiest Army parody I have ever heard. To see them doing it so daintily, believing they were singing something lovely, was a scene that I shall remember the rest of my life. I will never forget the strange look on the faces of the dignitaries, who were too polite to interfere.

The journey continued by train, then boat – to Iwakuni, Okinowa, and those small Paradise Islands where the Kamikaze suicide pilots spent their days before they plunged headlong to their death.

It was cherry blossom time, a most beautiful season. Each lunch hour and after work, the Japanese would take their food and saki high up on the mountains and then come down after dark with lanterns lit. Their coloured lights, together with the blossom, made a wonderful scene.

We went on to Hiroshima, where the devastation was almost unbelievable. I saw one victim of the A-bomb – and in the circumstances he could hardly be criticised – collecting money from sightseers for a look at his body.

On to Korea. Pusan. If ever there was a place entitled to be called the rat hole of the world, this was it. Desolation, squalor and mud. That's all it seemed to be. But surprisingly business went on as usual.

Before leaving England, I mentioned over the radio and TV that I was going to Korea and I would act as postman to anyone who wanted me to take a letter to their relatives serving out there.

There was some argument as to whether I was entitled to carry "mail" – it was, after all, the Royal Mail – this was resolved and I was allowed to do so, for the letters were posted to me anyway, enclosing the letter to be taken.

I also went with reporter status for the *Sunday Dispatch*, to send articles back describing the situation of displaced persons. As far as could be ascertained, there were about ten million displaced persons of which two million were orphans. Everything was arranged for me to visit the orphanages. First I was taken to the American orphanage at

Pusan. There was a huge board outside proclaiming that it was Hell's Garden American Orphanage and I must say that the Yanks did the kids proud.

Then I went to the British orphanage where I received a jolt, for staring at me was a board which read:

ILSIM ORPHANAGE
AND RUBBISH DUMP

I confess that at first I was angry to see this, because I felt that even though they were Korean children, it didn't seem fair to include them in the same bracket as a rubbish dump. I said so, in no uncertain terms, to the officer in charge.

He patiently allowed me to let off steam, and when I'd finished, he said quietly.

"Well, you see old chap, we do this because we want to do it. There is no money or goods set aside for this sort of thing. We simply do what we can," he pointed to the offensive board — "That board out there. It's there for a reason. You see, if we put some tins of corned beef, some loaves of bread and some planks of wood and the natives took them, that would be stealing — but if it's a rubbish dump..."

In a flash I realised that it was the British Army's way of getting around things.

I confess I felt a little ashamed of myself for blowing off steam, but at the same time I was rather proud of the way they had bent the rules.

At Eden Orphanage, where just two momma sans cared for twenty-two babies — laid out on the floor, by the way, because there were no other facilities for them, while the older children played outside — I met Tommy. Little Tommy couldn't have been much more than six years old, but he spoke English so well they made him Army interpreter.

The reward for his services was meals with the Army and he had two stripes stitched to his cap: both officers and men saluted him.

He had a perpetual grin and although he had been badly burned, he was a happy little chap who won everyone's heart.

A little girl at the camp wouldn't stop singing and the only song she knew was *God Save The Queen*. She could not have been more than four years old, and though she may not have been a Shirley Bassey, she received applause every time she sang it.

On we went up through to Seoul, then beyond to the 38th Parallel.

The Palladium seemed to be the favourite name for the shack built huts, which were erected as places of entertainment. It was near the 38th Parallel that we performed in one such place which leaned sideways. So much so, that it looked as though it would topple over. But it was cleverly conceived, for it was built on to the side of a mountain and tiers were cut away from the actual rising ground and this is where the lads sat.

This meant that when you walked on to the stage you were facing a wall of men so near you could almost shake them by the hand.

The weather got colder and colder as we went on.

Gloucester Valley. So silent, so grim, we saw the place where the gallant men had fought and realised just how hopelessly they had been trapped.

Before leaving England a Mrs Hilton of Heywood, asked me if I would try to locate her son's grave. I did, and not only took a photograph for her to keep, but also brought her some earth and some seeds of the flowers growing nearby.

By the time we got to the place known as Rear Div, it was freezing. We were taken to visit the men on duty at the top of a mountain called Kamuk San, overlooking the Imjin and the Chinese lines, and it really was incredibly cold.

Cold, or no cold, the show went on, and in the dressing rooms – one room separated by a blanket slung over a stretched piece of rope, the boys one side and the girls the other – we dressed and undressed.

In this intense cold, it was very difficult for our pianist to play because her fingers would hardly move, and a bowl of hot water was always called for. Somehow, though, we managed. They fitted us out with the same clothes as used by the Everest climbers – parkas and "long johns". Even the girls wore these and on one occasion in the finale, our singer stood looking lovely in her long evening gown. I said: "Show the boys what you've got on underneath," and she promptly lifted her dress to reveal her "long johns". The boys loved it.

My party consisted of Kay, the pianist, a brilliant musical entertainer, and a superb banjo player, known as Sonny Farrar. He used to be one of the stalwarts of the old Jack Hylton band. The other young lady was a dream. She was known for years in the business as Anna Mac. As a child performer, she was three times World Champion Scottish Dancer. Later she did an act playing the xylophone, then later as a singer and leading lady. If ever she reads this I hope she won't mind if I say she had the same appealing look and strident voice as Judy Garland, and as a comic's "feed", I never knew a better one.

No matter how tough the going, I never heard any one of them complain during the whole of the tour. They were super.

We didn't waste our time either, for apart from doing our shows and visiting orphanages, we left half-hour taped broadcast shows behind, so that they could remember after we had gone.

It was at Rear Div that we were housed in a hut with a very young boy to look after us named Cho Hyong Kee. He spoke excellent English. I have never met a more intelligent boy and I grew so fond of him that I wanted to adopt him.

He told me that he was proud to be asked, but since his parents had been killed, it was the money that he earned from the British Army that enabled him to pay for his younger brother and sister's education. Cho himself was

166

then only fourteen. He told me that he had to lie about his age to be employed by the British Army.

Cho used to sit and watch me type my articles for the *Sunday Dispatch* and was most impressed when the dispatch rider tore up to collect them and zoomed away again. As he was so fascinated with my portable typewriter, together with the fact that he not only spoke, but also wrote, very good English, I asked him if he would like me to leave it for him as a present when I left.

He was bashful and most excited. I told him I would do so if he promised to write to me. He agreed and kept his word, and although the machine must have fallen to pieces long ago, I still receive cards from him at Christmas time.

Cho, together with the Army lads had prepared a secret treat for us. They had been building a bath, and I was the first to have a soak bath in Rear Div. They had showers, of course, but this was different. This was to be the luxury of lying to soak in a specially made bath.

For this they had cut two large oil drums down the middle, long ways, and having knocked one end out of each, they put the two together and welded it which made it into a long bath. This was placed and piped to two large oil drums above, which contained water and a heating device. A string was attached to the tap, and on the special day, I had to strip off, climb into the bath, grab the string and pull and at the same time a great cheer went up. It soon turned to a peal of laughter – I was covered in red rust!

I have a sensitive skin anyway, and I can assure you that rust is not exactly the best of things to be smothered in. Apart from that I looked like a flaming Red Indian. As I streaked away to the nearest shower, I caught a quick glimpse of little Cho. He laughed so much I thought he was going to choke.

One little Korean lad was adopted by the Black Watch, and they took him with them wherever they went. When I met him I can't tell you how funny it was to see this almond eyed little Korean, talking English, with a Scottish accent.

The same thing applied to "Jackson". This was another young Korean, adopted by an American outfit. He was a little older, about twelve. After we visited them and he kissed both our girls, he was so enamoured with them he paid us a visit much later just to bring them a bunch of flowers.

I came up against several strange things in Korea. It was the first place where I had ever seen a house built of *Harpers* magazines. I was used to seeing shops built of NAAFI boxes, but this was a new one on me. They take a magazine with a shiny surface and scrape mud from the rice paddy fields on one side, leaving it in the sun to dry. This forms a kind of large brick. Then with these bricks they actually build a small hut-like dwelling, with the shiny pictures and surface on the outside, which are resilient to the sun. Quite a novel idea I thought.

Then I noticed that the poppa sans – the Korean equivalent to our senior citizens – all looked alike. They all seemed to have the long grey drooping mandarin-style moustache and beard and all wore a uniform-style hat, something like a Welsh national costume hat. The poppa sans head gear however, has no top to it at all.

When I asked why this was, I was informed that as the poppa san had reached the age of retirement, he had naturally accrued all his knowledge and wisdom, and any golden thoughts, or pearls of wisdom, must be given freedom to pass on to others. Hence no top to the headgear.

Yet with this delightful custom, there was another which spoilt it for me. I was told that these same people, or at least some of them, believe that to beat a blue-eyed dog to death and eat it, would be a cure for tuberculosis.

I thought how strange it was that people who could have such gentle ideas concerning the wisdom that they could pass on without a top to their hat, could countenance such a dreadful idea about a blue eyed dog!

We hadn't long been in Korea when it was evident that everyone was using a particular word, which seemed to cover everything. It was scoshee – meaning "little of" or "more or less".

"Will you have a drink?"

"Oh scoshee!"

It was scoshee this and scoshee that – we were fascinated.

Being a small man, and playing the banjo, I nicknamed Sonny Farrar, Scoshee Banjo, which was a name that stuck to him wherever he went. This became so ordinary that after a while we thought nothing of it. Until we arrived in Tokyo.

Here the troops sat in the hall, and the Japanese were allowed to look in the windows to see the show. They weren't allowed to occupy any of our serving soldiers' seats.

The Japanese faces at the windows seemed to enjoy the show, except for the chatter, which they didn't understand. But when I announced Sonny as Scoshee Banjo they fell about with laughter. I couldn't understand why. I learned later that Banjo is the Japanese name for their smallest room.

Poor Sonny, we played a nasty one on him at the custom shed.

Anyone who has travelled out East knows what bargains can be bought. Watches, cameras, binoculars and the like.

Sonny was no different to any of us and bought about five watches for various friends and as each day went by kept trying to convince himself that he wasn't going to declare them. Every day he thought he had found a different hiding place that was safe.

"I've got a great idea Charlie," he told me one day. "I'm going to strap a couple of the watches inside my actual banjo, they won't bother to unscrew all that, so I reckon that's a good place for two of them. Then if I have one on my wrist, and the others in various places, I don't see why I should declare them, do you?"

"Of course not Sonny. Mind you, if they catch you . . ."

He looked worried for a while and then later said: "Well, if I just declare one and make it look normal . . ."

"That's a good idea Scoshee. You'll get away with it."

This kind of chatter went on from day to day and he decided that he wouldn't declare any of the watches.

When we arrived at the customs shed he squared his shoulders, full of apprehension, and just as he neared the Excise man, the whole of our company stood together and, in a loud whisper, said: "Tick, tick, tick, tick, tick, tick."

He went straight up to the man and blurted out: "I've got five watches!" What he called us was strictly musicians' language!

Leaving the desolation of Korea I came away with a picture in my mind of a shell scarred wilderness with bombed cities interspersed, and at intervals in this dirty, ragged, brown waste, there would be an army camp. The flag pole would be surrounded by white stones. All would be neat and tidy. The parade ground and sports pitch would be cleared of all bits of waste paper. Everything was polished. The nissen huts, which housed the men, even had their little front gardens, sometimes only a yard square, but they looked like a miniature suburbia amidst all this rubble.

Somehow, although like any other soldier I hate "bull", it certainly made me feel proud to see the difference between our way, and theirs.

It's hard to tell what does bring happiness,
poverty and wealth have both failed.

CHAPTER EIGHT

Keeping up appearances is one thing,
keeping up your spirits – is everything.

IN the entertainment world, it's the people in your life that
make your life, and the shows in your life that make a
career, and the folks I have met have been so many and
varied that I have never found it dull. Naturally, being a
performer, most of my life long pals have been in, or connected with the business in some way.

Few people could claim to have found a friend in Beryl
Formby – George Formby's wife – yet somehow she took
to me.

George and Beryl arrived to top the bill at a special Army
show in Salisbury, in which I was appearing.

We got on like a house on fire. George told me at the time
that he wished he could find a good film script for himself,
and I offered to write one. I came up with an idea called

Rag Time Cowboy George. He went overboard for some of my ideas and later, at his flat in Baker Street, while the blitz was on, during my leave, I read the completed script to him.

He took delight in showing me his proudest possessions, dozens and dozens of the world's most expensive pens and watches – Vashrun and Constantines, Movados – which must have been worth a fortune. He told me that the only thing he couldn't get was a bottle of whisky and I managed to get him one. It cost me £3 – more than a week's pay to me – and he never paid me for it!

Zip Goes a Million, was a musical which suited George like a glove, but unfortunately he suffered a heart attack, which caused him to leave the show. A number of comedians followed on in his place, Reg Dixon, Roy Barbour and Jerry Verno were three that I remember. I took over from Jerry Verno.

When I got to Manchester, I received a call from George saying that he and Beryl would like to come over and see the show. I naturally said they would be welcome and where would they like to go for supper afterwards.

"Where do you normally go?" asked Beryl.

"Well, I usually go to the Koh I Noor, I love hot curry."

"Oh, that's marvellous," she replied, and went on to tell me that she and George liked it hotter than anyone. "You couldn't like it hotter than we have it," she insisted.

I rang the restaurant, and being a regular there, the Indian gentleman was very obliging. I wanted him to bring us a curry that was so hot, it would melt cuff links if they were too near it, and ignore the order placed at the table. "Very, very hot . . . yes indeed," he agreed.

True to his promise, he disregarded my table order and brought us a vindaloo that would have burned asbestos. I watched George and Beryl closely. Having said how hot they liked it, they daren't complain, and before the meal was half over we all sweating like demons, smiling sweetly and saying: "Delicious!"

It was in Southport, whilst I was playing *Zip Goes a*

Million at the Garrick, I filled in some of my spare time riding a hack along the beautiful miles of sandy shore.

One morning I was accompanied by our leading lady, Pam Beasley, and as she galloped past me, a piece of sand or something must have kicked up into my horse's eye. He bucked and leaped around like a mad thing, and although I was a competent horseman, he finally had me off, and with one foot still caught in the stirrup, he bolted, dragging me along. The result for me was an eyelid half torn off and a broken wrist.

The horse made its own way home and I passed out. Some very kind people took me to the hospital where they reduced the swelling and put on a plaster. I only missed the matinee. Being a Formby vehicle, though, I had to play the ukelele and doing so with a broken wrist was just about the most painful thing I have ever done. It made me sweat so much that the plasters wouldn't dry and in all I had seven plasters on that wrist. Although it finally knitted, it did so leaving a permanent lump.

Ah well, the show must go on they say.

Twice in my theatrical life I have had cause to admire someone who stood by this axiom, in adversity.

The first was Sylvia Welling, the soprano, who won such acclaim singing with James Etherington. These two had the romantic singing spots in my show *Sky High* at the Opera House, Blackpool for the season.

The show itself was a real George and Alfred Black extravaganza, with the Gang and myself, the Bernard Brothers, Harrison and Fisher, two sensational dancers from America, Tillers, show girls, specialities and scenic effects that were breathtaking.

Opening night – the show a sensation, and at the end, when the curtain came down, James Etherington walked to his dressing room, which was next door to mine and I thought he was clowning, pretending to be drunk. We all laughed at his antics and then popping next door to ask him something I saw him on the floor almost foaming at the mouth.

I lifted him gently, made him comfortable on the settee and sent for the doctor. The poor man had suffered a cerebral haemorrhage, and by the early hours of the morning he was dead.

Poor Sylvia, after having worked with him all those years, suddenly she was alone – the songs, the rehearsals, the orchestrations, all in vain now. Sylvia herself was like a person in a dream. It was so sudden, so unexpected, for Jimmy was young and something like a Douglas Fairbanks of the singing world. Sylvia insisted that she would go on.

Among my Gang was a tenor who had scored very heavily as a solo singer, Frederick Ferrari. He was called in urgently that morning and all day they rehearsed together and the show went on.

We were all very sad, but we had a great admiration for the lady who, with all her experience, sang tender loving duets with a comparative newcomer as though they had been doing it for years. Each song, each note, and each word must have been breaking her heart.

The other occasion was a little later, a voice I heard in the chorus of the show *Zip Goes a Million*, made the hairs on the back of my neck stand up. It was beautiful. I took the young lady aside and asked her name. It was Gladys Wilkinson. Not to my mind a good stage name, but a voice I was certain that would go far.

For three weeks I had her on stage every morning rehearsing and listening to a record of Annie Frind, singing the Nuns' Chorus from *Casanova*. I wanted her to copy the style of this singer, which she did. I gave her the name of Marian Miller, and she was principal vocalist in many of my television shows.

One morning on which we were due to do a live broadcast, I received a message from her aunt in Whitley Bay, that her father had just died. I was torn between telling her then, or leaving it until after the broadcast.

The dreadful thing being that she had to sing a song entitled *Oh My Beloved Father*, and strangely enough, the only other

174

orchestration available in her key, was a song called *Oh Mein Papa*. I decided that such a personal matter should not be kept from her for the sake of the show, and I quite expected her to withdraw from the broadcast.

I walked her round Hyde Park and broke the news to her as gently as I could, knowing that she had no mother, and that her father meant so much to her. She was distraught. I did let her know that there was no obligation for her to sing that day, especially in view of the song itself. She insisted that she would carry on, and although she almost collapsed after the broadcast, she went through it without breaking down.

Poor Marian, I once took her to lunch with Johnny Spitzer, the very portly young manager of the Sheffield theatre. He was an avid fan of all singers, but mostly for an American singer, who at that that time I had never heard of. Hour after hour in his office, the room would reverberate with song, for he constantly played the same singer, over and over again, and kept saying: "This man is the greatest I've ever heard."

It was a good prediction, for the man's name was Sammy Davis Jnr.

But on the day of the luncheon I drove Johnny and Marian out to a rather nice little country restaurant and just after the meal Marian suddenly doubled up with stomach pains. She went as white as a sheet and I offered to run her back to her hotel.

I told her to lay down on the back seat of my car, cover herself with her fur coat to keep warm, and that as soon as I'd paid the bill I'd drive her back. I hurriedly paid the bill and when I got to the car there she was, stretched out on the back seat. I drove as fast as I could, for I knew that I could get some medical attention to her at the hotel.

As we were half way up the hill approaching Sheffield, Marian let out a series of moans and shrieks and I stopped the car, opened the back door, and tried to comfort her. Just as she was lying there in agony, with me talking to her from the doorway, a young boy cyclist pulled alongside, jumped off his bike, stared at her and asked what the trouble was.

In a flash I grabbed him, and I don't know why, but I said: "Quick . . . she's due to have the baby any second now, so will you stay and deliver it, or will you go for the water?" The poor kid went whiter than Marian. He stiffened at the thought and shouted: "Goodness no. I'm not stopping here, I'll go for the water."

Whether he came back with the water or not, I don't know but he jumped on the bike and pedalled away as if he had a horde of demons after him.

Marian wasn't in any position to enjoy the joke, but I must confess the look on that boy's face and the way he pedalled away, has kept me amused ever since.

Apart from my show business friends, I have met others too, who, though not in the business, would dearly love to have been. Lovable extroverts like Bob Jones, the Welsh tobacconist at Bangor, who always kept a few fags "under the counter" when they were scarce. He was stage struck, and at the drop of a hat, he would don a straw boater, pick up a cane, and sail straight into *Sarah, Sarah, Aintcha Comin' Out Tonight.*

The same could be said of another successful business man, George James. He had several thriving businesses ranging from scrap metal to furniture shops, and was the first person to be granted a licence to open a casino in the country. Yet at heart, he was a frustrated performer. I am sure he would have given it all up for the chance to "tread the boards".

When I was booked to appear for him at his cabaret in the Casino at Port Talbot, I did a long performance, and still he kept finding reasons to make me do further encores, including presenting me with cuff links on the floor, so that he could at least be on the floor with me.

After that performance I had to go to the big steel works and do a show there. George insisted on coming with me. The only thing was that while I was on the floor working, he was sitting at a table knocking back the drink, and he finished up sloshed to the gills and wanting me to go into partnership with him.

John Street, a friend of mine, and one of the most generous men in the world to charities, has been making and exporting record players and such things for years, and yet he has confessed to me several times that he would have preferred to have been a mediocre performer, than a successful business man.

John was made a Companion of the Grand Order of Water Rats and in his own way is able to bring a great deal of pleasure to the people of show business he loves so much. So in that respect, he is "one of us".

Then there was one of the greatest extroverts I have ever known at Chiswick. He was a bookmaker called Jimmy Knode, a real fan of variety who never missed coming to the old Chiswick Empire. He always wore an enormous rose in his button hole and his letter headings proclaimed the fact that Jimmy Knode was the man who always wore a rose.

When I arrived at Chiswick Empire, I went to my dressing room and there on my make up place was a large bottle of champagne with an unusual label. It was a printed label bearing his photograph complete with shiny top hat and rose in the button hole. It read: "Welcome to Chiswick. Jimmy Knode."

He practically lived in my dressing room and was often known to buy the front two rows for people who could ill afford to go, not only to the Chiswick Empire. He also often bought the two front rows at the Palladium. To have his name mentioned, was the nearest he came to performing, but this seemed to be his way of getting as close to it as possible.

It's funny, but when you start to get analytical about things you come up with some strange results. For instance, it seems odd to me that most of the men who play the gruesome parts, are usually the most soft and gentle types. Although I have never met Vincent Price, he certainly does

177

exude charm and above all a delightful sense of humour.
I did meet and work once with Arthur Pratt, better known as
Boris Karloff and a more soft spoken, gentlemanly creature,
you could never wish to meet. And Peter Lorre, the villain
in so many films, had the most sympathetic manner of them
all.

Come to think of it, my neighbour, Peter Cushing, is of the
same mould, soft spoken, studious and a very gentle soul.

Taken a step further it also seems odd to me that most of
the great singers of this world, especially tenors, all seem to
come from mountainous countries: Italy, Scotland, Ireland,
Germany. Wherever there are mountains, great tenors
seem to be produced.

In the field of comedy it would seem that funny men
from the North outnumber those from the South by at least
ten to one.

Liverpool in particular would seem to be the home of most
comics. Charlie Olden came from there, he changed his
name to Nedlo, which is Olden in reverse, after which he
became the one and only Ted Ray.

Arthur Askey is another, Ken Dodd, Tommy Handley
and so many more. I have often wondered why this is so.
Tommy Handley was probably the greatest of all the radio
script reading comedians. *It's That Man Again* became an
institution.

I think perhaps one of the most rewarding remarks made
about me by Tommy Handley, was in a show where someone
mentioned my name, and jokingly Tommy replied: "Don't
mention the name Charlie Chester to me."

To which they said: "Oh a thing like that only happens
once in a lifetime."

Tommy said: "Yes, but why did it have to be my lifetime?"

Only a joke I know, but a flattering one.

Some time later, Tommy and I were both on a midnight
matinee show for charity, in his home town, and the following day we had to attend a cricket match.

When we both appeared on the scene, the crowd suddenly

178

took off and made for us in a mad swoop, thousands of them. We ran, and as we did so, Tommy yelled: "You go that way Chas, I'll go this." We split, and I remember thinking that at last I had "made it" for the crowd broke into two sections and I noticed that half were after me and half chasing him.

When Tommy died, the BBC later offered me his contract.

After we had been together doing non-stop crazy shows and broadcasting for six years, the Gang started to get restless. Some of them wanted the chance to become stars in their own right. With six years in uniform together and six years on the tours, they had certainly done their apprenticeship, and although I felt that we could have become an "institution", I had no right to deny them the opportunity of "making it" on their own.

We broke up.

I was now back as a single, and in a position to either do solo variety spots, or formulate a new gang.

I decided to go it alone for a while. I headed my own "Variety" bills and was careful to choose the kind of acts that could also "muck in" and do some comedy bits with each other.

Business in those days was still fairly good. In fact only one place I recall opened to bad business, and I hit on an idea. I had an insurance policy pinned to a notice board outside the theatre announcing: PATRONS FOR THAT WEEK WERE INSURED AGAINST DEATH BY LAUGHING. After that we played to packed houses. Variety. The spice of life . . . and it was.

I also did literally hundreds of broadcasts. *Workers' Playtime; Variety Bandbox; Variety Ahoy; Alhambra of the Air; Variety Playhouse* – so many I've lost count.

I also devised a new show for myself, *Keep Smiling*, which ran for a very long time. Then another *Come To Charlie*, and after that *A Proper Charlie*. Guesting for Bob Monkhouse and Denis Goodwin, Henry Hall, Bebe and Ben and a host of other shows, kept me busy with new scripts all the time. Later I went into television with a new idea, the very first TV give-away show *Take Pot Luck*, which ran for years.

I also wrote a full length musical, which Eric Maschwitz liked and it became an hour and half programme on TV entitled *A Sparrow in Fleet Street*.

I tried my hand at Shakespeare and played Bottom in *Midsummer Night's Dream*. I also went into farce and took out such shows as *Done in Oils, Just the Ticket, Boeing Boeing, Big Bad Mouse*, which all added to my experience.

I paid particular attention to TV and was contracted for two years, with a further option for two years and so on.

Charlie Chester Music Hall; Red Peppers, with the delightful Eleanor Summerfield, who played my wife. We seemed to be such a natural that from *Red Peppers*, we went for two series with a show called *The Two Charlies*, based on the mishaps of a couple of touring pros.

Educated Evans was a long-running show on TV that came out of my suggestion to Ronnie Waldman (who at that time was Head of Light Entertainment) that the BBC should obtain the rights to Edgar Wallace's book, *Educated Evans*, so I could rewrite it as a musical. This, of course, would only have meant one showing, with perhaps a repeat. But after obtaining the rights, Ronnie told me that as they had been so successful with a half hour show called *Dixon of Dock Green*, would I like to do it as a weekly half hour show?

Sydney Nelson and Maurice Harrison wrote some delightful scripts and this show had top rating from start to finish.

It was during the run of this two year show that I met many straight actors, who from week to week, appeared in guest parts.

Pat Hayes, who later became the woman artiste of the year for her marvellous performance in *Edna the Inebriate Woman*, was one of the resident cast, with Michael Balfour, Jack Melford and Keith Pyott. Visiting stars included such people as Sidney Tafler, Fabia Drake, Alfie Bass and Sid James.

180

Sid was most unnerving; he would arrive for the first rehearsal word perfect, and while we were ploughing around with scripts in our hands learning it, he would be standing there waiting for his cue. Apparently he had taped the script and learned it all before he arrived.

Alfie was quite different; he would spend all week learning a script and then deliver different cue lines on the show.

One particular artiste sticks out in my mind as one of the most convincing I have ever worked with – Ian Fraser, who played an old Bailey judge on one occasion.

I stood in the dock pleading on behalf of a certain "Sniffy Connor", a petty thief, and the conversation went something like this.

"Please don't send 'im up your royal worship, he's a good lad really."

"Don't call me your royal worship!"

"No your grace, only as I said, he's very good to his missus."

"Really? Well how is it that his last four convictions have been for wife beating?"

"Well you know how it is!"

"I do *not* know how it is!"

At this point there was a noise as one of the studio men dropped something, and as the audience tittered, Ian, the judge, resplendent in his red robes, forgot the script and ladled into the offending technician, and the audience, saying that this was a court of law, and that he couldn't conduct a case in a beargarden.

His face became so florid it almost matched his robes, and although it was the first time I had seen a straight actor ad lib, it certainly made the whole scene come to life and really seem true.

I have found it an impossibility to list some of the events of a lifetime in chronological order, and digging back into the caves of the mind, it doesn't seem to matter. They just pop up like stones, some precious and some just stumbling blocks.

There are some that are large enough to sit and dwell on, and others that are tiny marbles that roll around the courtyard of consciousness, but whatever their dimension or shape, they form a kaleidoscope of contentment to look back on.

Listening as I did, many years ago, to Bruce Seton as *Fabian of the Yard* I never realised what great friends we would become. We actually met as members of the Lords Taverners.

Bruce was a man of culture and had a delightful sense of humour, he loved variety performers.

His sister married Lord Tedder and she became very involved in the RAF Malcolm Clubs. These were the social clubs of the RAF named after their first VC.

Having already been to Germany for him, Bruce asked me if I would do another one-night stand for the RAF. I naturally agreed but I was rather shaken, when he said: "That's fine old boy, I'll book your flight."

"Where is it then?" I asked.

"The Astra at Bahrein," he replied, as if it were just round the corner.

He told me that Lord Tedder and his sister were quite fond of me and that when they were on holiday on one of the remote islands of Scotland, they were visited daily by a seal. It was such a friendly little chap, they called it by my name, and conversely, they always referred to me as "the Seal".

This also reminds me of the time when the BBC were 'all at sea,' for although my Gang and I had recorded our weekly programme at Blackpool I suddenly received a message saying that they had 'lost it'. Where the half hour show disappeared to is a complete mystery to this day. Somehow I had to find all my boys and the leading lady and get them together to do it all over again, quickly. Henry Hall's band was available, but only for that afternoon, which meant I only had a short time to find them all. I had messages flashed on cinema screens. The leading lady was found shopping, some of the lads were on the golf course, and by the grace of God I managed to find them all in time.

It was this that changed Frank Chacksfield's way of life, for instead of remaining my musical arranger and backroom boy, he now had to take the baton and become the conductor. He has since become a great name in his own right, with his own particular brand of music, and I feel very happy to have been his starting off point.

Recordings are things that were not often lost by the BBC but there was a time when two of their artistes were hopelessly lost.

With a very happy and successful broadcast in *Henry Hall's Guest Night* from the Alhambra, Bradford, completed, the announcer and I went with Henry, back to his hotel for supper. We had both been fixed up in the same digs for the night, and weren't in any hurry to get back there.

The blackout was still in force at the time, and during supper the town experienced one of the fiercest gales it had known for years, and the rain was torrential. We left Henry to find our digs, and after walking for a long time, we realised that not only were we lost, there was no chance of finding the address, for the blackness prevented seeing where we were, and lighters and matches were hopeless in the high wind.

We suddenly saw a telephone box in the distance and ran towards it filled with hope. Alas, all we had were half crowns and coins that were no use for phoning. We finally found the railway station, and tired, wet, we boarded a train there, in an effort to get our of the wet and the wind.

We both fell asleep and awoke in Crewe . . . What a night!

I often wonder if the announcer Mark White, now Head of Radio 2, remembers that awful night.

There were lots of awful nights for most of us during the war, and yet for one young lady it was meant to be a night of happiness.

183

My show was routed to Honiton in Devon to entertain a
rather large audience of ATS and Land Army girls. What an
audience they were, they laughed so loud and long, they
made us laugh. One of the things that tickled them was the
balloon dance that I did as a young lady with long flowing
black hair with gardenias, and saucepan lids on elastic for
for my bra, and Eddie le Roy (Eddie Gray's younger brother)
as the cave man, with tiger skin leotard and red hairy tights.
We looked funny enough, and when we did the dance in
serious vein, the laughter mounted.

Suddenly there was a shriek, it was different to the other
laughter, and we naturally cocked an ear. This caused the
young lady concerned to explode even worse, and then, we
heard it – water! There was quietness for a split moment, and
we all realised that she was wetting herself and she couldn't
stop.

We all laugh at other people's misfortunes and the poor
girl must have been terribly embarrassed. When everyone
realised what was actually happening, the whole piace
erupted afresh, and sad to say, the poor girl, who was
enjoying herself so much, fainted and had to be carried out
on a stretcher.

The top man in a show is usually the one everybody goes
to when there is trouble, or something to be decided. A
common occurrence used to be one of the dancing girls
fainting, they were automatically taken to my room for a lie
down until they felt better. During rehearsals for a TV show,
one of the Leslie Roberts girls suddenly screamed. She had
kicked sideways and her leg was stuck; she was in agony.

As luck would have it, I have always been interested in the
human body. Two of my in-laws were osteopaths, and having
been in the Sea Cadets I had learned the rudiments of first
aid. However, this didn't cover bones out of place, which
this girl obviously had. Somehow I knew what to do, or
thought I did, and everyone was looking to me for some
immediate action.

I took her into a side room, and asked one of the other

girls to accompany us, because I didn't want her to come out of that room with only me there, crying her eyes out. I got her on to the table tennis table, kneeling down with her bottom towards me, and being a slight little thing I was able to grab her hips, one in each hand, and wrench them open. There was a kind of "thump" as the hip went back into position, and although she gave one hell of a shout and renewed her tears, she got off the table and walked out of the room normally.

A similar thing happened when I was working on a cruise, in a ship called the *Stratheden*. I think I worked harder on that ship than anywhere else. I was originally the cabaret, but after a while, I was lecturing, visiting the sick, organising games, old-time sing songs, forming a ship's choir, and so on. Pirate night in Frenchman's Cove in the Caribbean, saw me making up ladies as pirates with moustaches, and even putting flesh make up on parts of the body which didn't conform with others that had been exposed to the sun.

On this trip I met two of the nicest people I have ever known Sir Geoffrey and Lady Hulton. Why they took to me I'll never know, but they did, and Geoffrey, who had a pretty rough time during the war, had had to retire early.

"Charlie, you'll look after Patti for me won't you?" he would say, and looking after Patti was a pleasure indeed. She was an extremely good conversationalist and full of fun.

Dancing one night, however, she suddenly tottered back to me as white as a sheet and limping so badly, she could hardly walk at all. The following day she was worse, and Geoffrey was very concerned.

Patti asked me if I would treat her as a twisted ligament in her leg was absolute agony. I explained that I was in no way qualified, but that I was prepared to do whatever I could.

They came together to my cabin, and I gave her a massage explaining all the muscles and the bones as a prelude, and to make her drowsy. I then began to treat her groin and there was a ligament like a cord, which seemed to be twisted.

Geoffrey, with complete trust, sat there and read the paper.

After I had given her treatment for about thirty minutes, all seemed well, and I advised her to take a nap, after which she would enjoy a cold shower. She slept for about twenty minutes, and then got up and took her shower and walked out of my bathroom singing as if nothing had ever been wrong. She was delighted.

I can also remember the time when I could have done with a massage myself, following a rather hectic period on a horse. The organiser of the Jersey Battle of Flowers, wrote and asked if I would head their parade on a horse. I accepted with great pleasure, for there's nothing I like better than straddling a horse, and the idea intrigued me.

I was to ride at the head of a large procession of colour and noise, directly behind the Queen's coach. The Queen that year was Petula Clark.

I dressed for the occasion in Western attire, resplendent in filigreed leather chaps and gay coloured shirt, and the largest ten gallon hat of pure white. I was introduced to my horse.

It wasn't particularly keen on the event from the start, but I mounted and walked it up and down for a while. We got to know each other . . . well not exactly to know each other because on my side it was respect, and on the animal's side, it was more liked hatred.

They didn't tell me that the animal had a dislike for music, and when the band, or at least one of them, lined up directly behind us, my partner decided to perform his idea of the Gay Gordons. This didn't exactly worry me, but instead of looking like a smart cowboy, my shirt started to come out at the back. and I looked distinctly rumpled, and the band hadn't even tuned up yet.

Pet Clark looked every inch a Queen, in her coach be-decked with flowers. She took up her position in the front and my horse took a fancy to the greenery confronting him. As soon as the parade moved off, my animal friend tried to prove what he was by his actions, without me being told.

A racehorse! What's more he was determined that this was one race he really could win. So apart from trying to hold him back from sprinting the parade, together with the fact that I was denying him the green refreshment he fancied, so invitingly near his nose on Pet's coach, we now had the added harassment of the band blasting Sousa's decibels up its derriere. This wasn't his idea of fun at all. To keep him amused and to let him enjoy a little of the fun, I allowed him to edge near Pet's coach and nibble some of the fernery, and he might have settled for this, had not the object of the whole exercise begun. Namely, for all and sundry lining the route, to make as much noise as they could and bombard us with flowers. Petals, stalks, leaves, and even clods of earth, came flying through the air and I had a rodeo all to myself.

I really can't remember who perspired the most, the horse or me. I think it was me. I know one thing for certain, if ever I am asked to do it again, I'll make sure that my partner is in no way connected with the sport of kings.

Workwise, I remember too some of the early days of TV. In fact the very first time I stood in front of a camera was at Earls Court, Olympia. It was a closed circuit affair and we had to be made up by Max Factor girls in the window, so that people could see it being done. The face was a bright yellow, and the lips were almost black and the overall effect was to look something like Geronimo. We then performed underneath a boom arm microphone, in front of a camera and the pictures were seen on sets throughout the exhibition.

My next TV appearance was at Alexandra Palace, where there were two cameras only, one facing one wall, and the other facing the opposite wall at the other end of the long narrow studio. We performed to one camera, and then had to do a David Hemery, over all the cables, whilst changing, to the other end of the room and face the other way, so that the next shot could be taken. It was almost like being a human yo-yo. The technicalities of television, however, took

187

giant strides and soon there were cameras galore and bigger studios.

In one of my series I was asked to use the services of an American film star – a man who excelled in parts like an eccentric Russian Prince, or something of that ilk. I said at the time I would rather not have the onus of writing material for Mischa Auer, he needed specialist material and was used to Hollywood writers. Ronnie Waldman, told me that Mischa had been contracted for twelve weeks and that they had no other show in which to put him, so I had to have him. Ronnie then suggested that I go to see him perform at the theatre. I did, and I wasn't terribly impressed. His main trick was to play a piano by rolling two oranges up and down the keyboard. This might have been good except that he had been drinking rather heavily and he kept dropping the oranges.

I went back to Ronnie and asked if I could do my show without him.

"Go and see him once more Charlie," he said.

I did, and it was a similar experience. He was great as an actor with a good script and a marvellous comedy character, but he was no music hall man, and I had doubts about him fitting in with my show.

Ronnie asked me how it went.

"He was drunk I'm afraid, and I'm very worried," I replied.

"All right then, I'll tell you what," said Ronnie. "He is due to report for rehearsals on Monday in Praed Street. Now, *if* he turns up drunk, he has broken his contract and you needn't bother, but if he turns up sober, I'm afraid you'll have to write him in."

"OK." I agreed, fervently hoping that Mischa would arrive half cut.

He turned up as sober as a judge, very polite and most affable, and with a face as mournful as a bloodhound he asked for his script.

Up until then, I hadn't written a word for him. I got

188

cracking and during rehersals knocked him up some parts in the show. I had one idea for the finale, and that was to have each performer, each act, walk down at the end to the camera and apologise to the audience saying something like: "Don't blame me, I'm only a dancer!" or something similar, leaving me to take the entire blame for the show as the last one down.

Mischa, as the principal guest, naturally preceded me. At the time the big news was that an American admiral had been made supremo over the British admirals. The line I gave him to say was "Don't blame me, and I think your British admirals are marvellous." Then, for no rhyme or reason, as he delivered the line (which at that time might easily have got him a round of applause) he decided to hold his nose, and raise his other hand, as if pulling the chain, and lowered himself out of vision. Thousands of letters came with a storm of protest. How *dare* that American say and *do* such a thing.

Ronnie Waldman saw me later. He was very sympathetic, but said: "I know . . . Just do your best Charlie,"

At least I now had something to work on. In the following show I wrote him four spots to himself. The first was a comedy routine of reading some of the letters, castigating him for what he did. The second was a similar shot, only this time there were so many letters that he was almost buried beneath them, and the postman comes in and says: "If you think that lot is bad, wait until you read this lot," and they threw another couple of sacks full over him.

It was beginning to gel now, the audience liked him. The next shot was of a naval squad arriving to arrest and escort him to the Admiralty. The last shot was of Mischa profusely apologising to a British admiral, and tall though the American was, the British officer towered above him. There was an exchange of repartee, after which the British admiral offered to settle the affair with "coats off out the back," and Mischa almost begging for mercy.

This is where the camera should have tracked back

revealing the fact that the tall British admiral was, in fact, a tiny midget, standing on a step ladder. Unfortunately the camera didn't track back, so the whole sequence was never really understood by the viewers.

I took pains earlier to tell of the hardships I suffered through being branded as a young Max Miller, and it would only be fair to say what joy I had in being vindictive, in a very minor way. Looking back it was pretty childish of me, and yet, at the time it made me feel good.

Julia Golden, the agent asked me if I would share top of the bill with Max at one of her Sunday concerts at the Casino in London.

I was to close the first half of the bill and Max was to take top spot on the second half. Before the show opened, however, one of the stage hands came across and said: "Max wants to know if you'll change places with him and let him go on the first half, so that he can get back to Brighton?"

After all those years of misery and frustration, here he was asking me to do him a favour. I sent a message back to him. "If Max wants me to change places with him, let him come and ask me himself, and not send a stage hand."

He did. He said, "Would you mind Charlie, only I'd like to get back to Brighton?"

I said: "Not at all Max, it'll be my pleasure." It was too. A pleasure to know that I was able to follow him, for after all, even though I had no personal love for him, I shall always regard him as the greatest front-cloth comic ever.

It's strange how 'touchy' some of the great impressarios can get over silly little things. I don't know whether it was because Val Parnell had married an American or not, but he took exception to the most simple of jokes.

I had to follow a long list of American appearances at the Palladium – Mickey Rooney, Carmen Miranda, Danny Kaye, – and I joked: "They've had so many American acts here they don't have a stage manager, they have a deputy sheriff."

He didn't like it and asked me to take it out.

Mickey Rooney had an unfortunate stay in this country. He started off badly by going to see the show that was on prior to his own appearance, and sat in the box with his boots up on the ledge.

He left England three days before schedule, hiding what looked like an enormous black eye.

In his show, however, he raved about the comedy genius of one of our most loved comedians, Jimmy James. Mickey told his audience that this man was the funniest man he had ever met and that he was taking him back to the States with him. We all guessed that this would bring even more fame and fortune to our own Jimmy and it naturally got a storm of applause. Jimmy said nothing, and waited.

When my show followed some weeks later, I had a phone in the footlights which kept ringing and each time I would answer it and say: "No, not yet!" and put the phone down. This was a running gag, and at the end someone asked me who it was, to which I said: "It was Jimmy James. He wanted to know if there was any word from Mickey Rooney!"

As expected, Val asked me to take it out.

As Danny Kaye had been there some time before me and scored the biggest success of anyone, I had an idea which I thought might be good for a laugh. My idea was to have a tape made by Danny in America of a script, with spaces left on the tape, so that I could carry on a conversation with his 'ghost voice'.

I don't remember the actual script, but the concept was that as I stood cracking some gags at the mike, I would suddenly go into a part of his Minnie the Moocher routine and his voice would suddenly stop me, saying:

"Please don't do that Charlie."

I would look bewildered and stop.

"Yes, it's me, Danny Kaye."

"But Danny, you went back to America."

"Yes, I know, but don't you remember I always said that I would leave a part of me there, at the Palladium?"

191

"Yes, I remember you saying that Danny."

"Well Charlie, I wonder if you would do me a great favour?"

"Certainly Danny, anything!"

"Well, would you stand just where I used to?"

"Just here, like this?"

"That's right . . . and now would you put your hand out to the mike, like I did?"

"Like this Danny?" I put my hand out and held the mike.

"Yes, that's it . . . Now, would you run your hand up the mike stand to the top of it?"

"Yes Danny."

"Do you feel anything?"

"Yes, Danny I must confess, I feel a lump."

"Well, that's my chewing gum, you can have that."

This was to be a little throw away that I felt would have got a nice reaction, simply because the London Palladium audience were so fond of him. Unfortunately, Danny said it wasn't possible to make the tape recording owing to his contract. It was a pity, I still think it was a nice little piece.

I mentioned earlier about Danny being the biggest success there. Indeed I have never before seen people stand on their seats as they did at his farewell performance. Tears flowed and it was a night charged with emotion.

He came back to do a Command Performance when I had my show there. It was my second Command and my old mate Ted Ray was with me, which made me feel good. Although numbers one and two dressing rooms were mine all the week, on this particular night, naturally they have to house so many performers it's a case of share all round. I went to my room and found that the Crazy Gang had commandeered all the places in the large room and that Danny was by himself in the smaller room. Well, not exactly by himself, there was a man with a movie camera filming him making up.

Bud said to me: "There's no room here Charlie. You can't

192

expect to dress in the same room every night you know. You'd better go in there with "him".

I went in and asked if he minded me sharing the room as there was nowhere else, and my things were already in the wardrobe anyway. Without speaking a word, he moved a couple of things and just made space for me to make up. I almost felt as though I was using the wrong soap. Every so often I had to lean back so that the man with the camera could miss me and photograph Danny.

I went on in the first half for eight minutes only. Two more acts later Ted followed me and agreed that they were a very tough audience. Going back into the room I told Danny that they were a different audience to that he had played to on his last visit, and we had found them very hard going. He didn't seem very impressed, or talkative and I assumed that perhaps he had his own kind of "nerves".

His appearance was quite different this visit. His hair was very long, as he was in the process of filming *The Secret Lives of Walter Mitty*. He went on, and for the first ten minutes of his act he was fighting them. He won them over before the end, but the reception was nowhere the same as a normal variety audience.

When he came off, he sat on the divan by the window and pulled the wardrobe door open to hide himself, and sat there almost in tears. I was glad to retreat to the other room, where the Gang were in high spirits. Nothing could dampen the Crazy Gang.

It would appear to me that nearly all pros love sport, and nearly all sportsmen love pros. From the very first day I met Stanley Matthews, we took to each other. He was extremely shy and modest in those days and I think I helped him in some small way to overcome some of his modesty.

I noticed, being a house guest, that on Saturdays there was a constant flow of people knocking on the back door for tickets to the football matches – some paid for, others not, and his wife Betty was forever at the stove brewing up pots of tea.

The 'Maestro', the 'Wizard,' the 'Fox' – he was known as them all – was a difficult man to feed, and on match days it was mainly salads and vitamin pills. Not that he needed them, but he had a fetish for all the new vitamins that arrived on the market.

One Saturday, we were all going to the match and it happened to be Betty's birthday. Until then I had seen him display his wizardry many times, but I had never actually seen him score. I asked him if he would do so as a birthday present to Betty. He shrugged the whole thing off as a ridiculous joke, and yet, during the game he suddenly seemed to make up his mind and went through them all like a dose of salts, leaving four players on their backs having slid past them with his famous body swerve, then he let fly and scored.

The crowd went hysterical with pleasure and Stan casually looked up to where we were sitting and nodded as much as to say: "That's your birthday present."

It was while I was in Blackpool I organised what was the forerunner of today's Show Biz Eleven.

Stanley got together a team of retired players of note, interspersed with some current players and I made a team up of all comedians and performers. These were billed as ANCIENT LIGHTS versus COMICS UNITED.

What a match! The team were lined up to meet the mayor and then a giant of a horse was marched up and down between the teams, which was the first laugh. When I tell you that my team, plus reserves and assistants, included such names as Jewel and Warriss (sharing goal), Henry Hall (Manager), Norman Wisdom, Albert Modley, Jack Radcliff, Fred Ferrari, Arthur Haynes, Ken Morris, Nat Jackley, Jerry Desmonde, Jimmy Wheeler and Terry Thomas, it might serve to show you their strength, not as players, but as winners, for we made the Stanley Matthews eleven laugh so much, even they couldn't score much. It's true they won, but it was such a hilarious affair that I repeated it the following year and on each occasion we made over £1,700 for charity.

I then did the same thing in London, firstly at the Chelsea ground, in which Ted Tay, as a one-time football pro, played for me, and again at Queen's Park Rangers ground. This was perhaps the funniest one of all, for being in London, I had all the stars there and so many volunteered to play that we fielded one team for the first half and another for the second half. The best event of the day occurred after I had been informed that as they had finished their actual season, the club were proposing to plough up the pitch and re-lay it. The audience didn't know this and gasped when a tractor was driven across the ground from between one set of goal posts to the other, leaving great furrows behind it. It looked as if we had gone too far and several people almost fainted at the sight of what we had done.

Some years later I organised a match that was anything but funny – in fact I had practically every person, including Sir Stanley Rouse himself, shedding a tear of regret. This was the last match to be played by Stanley Matthews.

This took a great deal of organising, for we had some of the great players of the world come over to take part. All of these had not only to be insured, but also had to have an interpreter. People like Puskas, and the great Yashin of Russia, who could only speak through his interpreter, said it was an honour to come and play for the "Master".

I booked the Dagenham Girl Pipers for this great event; I had a reason for this, it was the fact that his wife Betty was a Scots girl and her father, Jimmy Vallance, was the man who found and fostered Stan in his early career. The lights went up on the pitch to a great roar, and then as the two teams of the world's greatest names in the game took the field, it reached a crescendo. I made Stanley stay behind with me at the tunnel, and after the teams had been piped into the centre of the field by the band, the Pipe Major returned to the tunnel, playing a lament. On reaching the tunnel she turned about and marched back to the other players, this time followed by the shuffling, embarrassed figure of Stanley. I saw the handkerchiefs flutter and unashamedly almost everyone I could see was weeping.

What a night it was.

I had twenty-two signed footballs dotted around the centre circle and at a given signal each player dribbled a ball to the outfield and kicked it into the audience as a souvenir.

They had some priceless signatures on them.

At the end of the game I had things well organised. The pipers took positions dotted around the field, and these were backed by scores of police, so that there would be no invasion of the pitch.

As the final whistle blew, the pipers marched in from various vantage points followed by the police, who made a circle round them, and in this way the players were encircled by the pipers, who in turn were encircled by the police. The pipers then played *Should Auld Acquaintance Be Forgot* and Stanley was lifted shoulder high as the lights dipped and the centre group were spotlighted. It was, I think, one of the most moving moments I have experienced.

But when it comes to shocks I think that television must take full credit, for this gave me one of the greatest shocks I can remember, and anyone who tells you that it's all pre-arranged, just doesn't know. When Eammon Andrews confronted me and said: "Charlie Chester, *This is Your Life!*" I went cold.

I had been at rehearsals all day at the television centre, and I had introduced a routine to Lionel Blair for his dancers. It was a routine of playing the spoons, not just clicking them, but a set routine which looked most effective. Learning the spoons, however, tends to give newcomers sore hands and bruises on their legs with the constant banging. The girls were very good though and practised ardently and were fast becoming very competent. It was a complete novelty for them anyway, and any break in the hard dance routine

196

was a welcome change. One girl, however, unknown to me, had been primed to be a bit dumb. She kept coming to me saying that she couldn't get one particular rhythmic movement. With patience I kept showing her, and I must confess that she acted her part very well.

Albert Stevenson the producer said we would knock off around six o'clock. At ten to six, however, I was asked if I would call in on Eric Maschwitz before I left. I did so, and after being with him for a while, I began to wonder why he had called me in, because he never said anything of importance. We chatted about the show and this and that, and I saw him go to the window and blow his nose. It never occurred to me then that he was giving a signal to someone.

The actors, like Felix Aylmer and hosts of others had all been asked to sit in the reception hall until that moment and then, as we came down in the lift, they would all make for the doors. This meant that we had to fall in behind all these famous names and follow them out.

I didn't even see the taxi from which the film was being taken, neither did I hear Eammon saying: "Among these actors and actresses, there is one man who will be coming out through that door in a moment having been rehearsing with his show."

The Head of Light Entertainment, Eric Maschwitz, and I walked out together and within a few paces I saw Eammon, lurking behind one of the great pillars.

I shouted to him. "Hi there Eammon. Working?"

He said: "Yes, on you . . . This Is Your Life."

Eric laughed and walked a few steps away and I remember shouting good naturedly: "Eric, you bastard!"

After the initial shock, I was more or less incommunicado until the show. It was a moving experience and a very upsetting one for me. What I didn't know at the time was that my wife, Dorita, knew, but being a pro she wouldn't have spoilt it for anything. She never breathed a word to me. I do remember I was going to rehearsals that day in some

197

THE WORLD IS FULL OF CHARLIES

old clothing and she said: "If you're rehearsing at TV Centre you should at least put a decent suit on."

My wife has always been fanatical about looking smart and having clean underclothes daily. If I wear a shirt for an hour, it's soiled, and she suggests that I change it. Both she and my son Peter kept the secret between them and when Peter went to play at some function in the evening, she made him wear his dress suit, thinking that he would be called, the same as herself.

They never were.

Something went wrong. I don't know what, but they by-passed her and my boy completely. They weren't invited, and after the show I rang home to Dorita who was quite put out about the whole thing. How, or why this happened I don't know, but it spoiled what was, a memorable occasion.

The important thing about getting somewhere
is the amount of happiness you achieve
when you've arrived.

CHAPTER NINE

The beauty of today is that if yesterday
was your enemy, tomorrow may be your
best friend.

WHEN it comes to name dropping, I admit to being as
guilty as anyone, but if it brings back a pleasant memory of
a meeting or an occasion, then I see no harm in it.

I often smile when I think of one occasion, when we, as
soldier entertainers, were performing at Windsor to an
audience including the Queen Mother, Queen Mary. Our
vocalist was Don Carlos, a handsome and popular singer,
and if there was one thing Queen Mary enjoyed it was the
community singing spot, which he handled.

Although the Queen mother enjoyed it she had a very
stern face during the performance and Don was petrified
in case he should do something wrong, but after singing two
songs he began to feel at home.

Suddenly, looking very grim indeed, the Queen glared up at him and beckoned him forward with her finger. Don was bewildered, and from the way he went white, anyone would have thought that he was destined to be shot at dawn. He stared back at her, and then looked to the next of us for support.

"What's up?" I whispered.

He looked at me, rolled his eyes upwards and nodded his head towards the front row, where he was still being beckoned to go forward.

"Well, don't just stand there, go down and see what she wants," I told him.

He bowed and scraped his way down the front steps and leaned forward to hear what she had to say. The silence was almost ominous. The sweat began to pour off Don.

He needn't have worried, for all she said was: "Young man, why aren't we singing *There Is a Tavern in the Town*?"

I can still see the look of relief on Don's face.

Queen Elizabeth, for whom I had already been in two Commands, also came with Princess Margaret and Prince Michael, to the pantomime *Jack and Jill*. At the interval, both Michael Bentine and myself, were invited to take tea in the royal box, and we were made so much at home that the curtain was late going up for the second half – and for once, Emile Littler didn't mind.

Another royal occasion for me was at Claridges Hotel, where I auctioned two of Princess Margaret's Siamese kittens for charity.

One of the great names in the world of photography was Baron and I used to go to him for my front of the theatre photographs and fan photos. He had a strange technique – or at least, so it seemed to me. He would have me leaping into the air, whilst he was taking shots lying on the floor, and a session with him was a bit too invigorating. Then I had to relax and it was during this period that the actual pictures were taken, almost without my knowing.

With Baron was another photographer, a pleasant fellow

called Anthony Armstrong Jones. It would appear to be quite a distinction to have one's photographs taken by both a Baron and a Lord.

I have never taken Lord Snowdon's photo, but at least I have had the pleasure of painting his portrait, and the proceeds of sale of this have purchased yet another chair-mobile for the handicapped, which he designed.

Prince Philip is a most interesting person to meet, he asks a lot of questions and likes to know how things work, and why things happen. He is also very quick with his repartee, even with us comics he can give as good as he gets.

Ted Ray and myself were given the very pleasant task of entertaining him for an evening, at what I believe was his first visit to a greyhound race meeting. The Prince was so interested in what went on, he even brought binoculars with him to watch the dogs loaded into the traps, and to see just how they were handled. He has a ready laugh, which is a magnet to a comic, and it was refreshing to find someone "topping" us for laughs. The Prince is a Companion of the Grand Order of Water Rats, and because of this, when he arrived in Plymouth to review the ships there, I was at the Hoe Theatre and I sent him a telegram saying "Welcome to Plymouth. Hope you enjoy your fish and ships." He replied "Thanks Charlie, wish you could be with us." I would have liked to, for with such an occasion, he killed our business for that day.

On another occasion I was invited to the Palace to attend the Duke's Award Scheme and as I stood with the large crowd he suddenly saw my Rat badge. "Ah, a Water Rat," he exclaimed and came over for a chat. This was about the time he had sustained a nasty fall from his polo pony and wrenched his shoulder. I asked him if it still hurt. He said. "A little. Stupid thing to do though."

I replied: "I don't know about stupid sir, I think polo's a good name for it – I thought you were riding the horse with the hole in the middle."

The press, on one occasion, overplayed a remark he made about the Royal finances, and at one of the Jack Solomons World Sporting Club dinners, I had to propose the guests, of which the Duke was guest of honour.

I shall never forget how he chuckled when I said that I hoped he was comfortable and not sitting in too much of an overdraft! At the time the Royal Family were being seen on television all over the world in a documentary about their daily activities. I had this in mind when I added: "I don't know why you should be worried about finances sir. From what I've seen, you've done a damn sight more on television than I have lately! I had visions of you opening a window at the Palace, throwing a bottle at one of the guards, and saying "*Shh*! you know who!"

He replied and gave as good as he had received and closed the subject by saying: "Regarding television, it's all right for you. *You get paid for it.*"

Having mentioned the press, my mind recalls with pleasure, the great affinity it has with the members of my profession. Every year at the Press Club they have a "Variety Night" to which they invite King Rat and the members of the Order. An impromptu concert is given after the dinner and on two occasions I saw Bransby Williams, then at a great age, give a performance of Dickens characters, that was absolutely marvellous. This man had magic. Of the writers and cartoonists, particular friends of the profession were Hannen Swaffer (who to me seemed rather choosey about his subjects), Bill Boorne, Bill McGowran, Tom Webster, Roy Ullyet, Jimmy Green, and now joining forces as a critic, my one time TV producer and friend, Richard Afton.

I always enjoyed the company, and indeed the articles of a great writer and journalist W. Connors, better known as Cassandra. The only time I didn't appreciate his article was when he wrote a vitriolic spate of venom at Liberace, for whatever Liberace is, or is not, he is a supreme artiste. He has never to my knowledge done anything to desecrate either his own, or the name of show business, and there are not many who have been more charitable.

Still, you can't win 'em all I suppose, and on the subject of winning, I am reminded of a TV Show I was invited to do by Barney Colehan. It was called *It's a Knock Out*. It was a new idea involving towns competing against each other in a series of light-hearted competitions. Ted Ray was in Yorkshire and would handle that county, and I was in Lancashire and compered that side of things.

It is hard to describe the antics they had to perform, such as seventeen people getting into a mini car and then drive it through obstacles.

When we got to Morecambe, there was one old boy with a stall, right in the middle of the acting area, on the sands. The BBC offered to "pay him for the day" but he wouldn't budge, so we performed all around him until he finally packed up and went home.

The one thing the organisers didn't work out though, was the time of the tides, and I finished up compering some of the things with the sea lapping up over my shoes. I was sad when Ted and I were dropped from the show, but it is good to know it is still as popular as ever and has even gone on to the Continent.

People's reactions to a challenge are sometimes rather strange. *Take Pot Luck*, which I devised, became the first give-away show on TV and had a very long run, both on the "box" and on the stage. When we played at Cardiff, a fine looking youth came on stage and competed in a simple comedy gimmick and won. I asked him what he did for a living and he replied: "I work down the pits" to which I suggested he would enjoy the fresh air, and went on to tell him that he had won a Roadmaster Hercules bicycle. He immediately said: "How the hell am I going to get that home?"

"Ride it," I suggested. "Where do you live? Wigan?"

On another occasion a woman won a television set, which was the top prize every week. As soon as I told her that she had won it, she exclaimed: "What about the aerial and the licence?"

I had a little problem over the TV set in Coventry. It was won by a little girl sitting in the gallery, who happened to be in a lucky seat. Then by just calling out the correct number from a series of envelopes, she chose the one that corresponded with that of the television. After the show the child was brought around by a woman who seemed very worried.

"You see," she started. "I brought my own little boy and our next door neighbour's little girl and during the show my boy was sitting next to me in that seat, but he had to leave in the interval, to go to his school swimming gala, so the little girl moved into his seat. This means that she got his prize."

In short, she was now claiming the girl's prize. I wanted no argument and suggested that whoever bought the tickets was entitled to the prize. But the mother of the little girl arrived and complained that I had given her little girl's prize to someone else.

I had a hard think and tried to assess the rights and wrongs of the situation and I reached the conclusion that whoever was sitting in the lucky seat at the time its number was called was the correct winner, especially as that person had nominated the correct envelope containing the prize. I suggested that to make thing simple, the two families sell the article, which was valued at about £73 and split down the middle. In this way they were both winners. I left the town on the Saturday and some weeks later heard from a solicitor that they had taken legal proceedings against each other. What foolishness!

I also had a nerve-racking moment at London's Victoria Palace, with the same show. This, however, was all in good fun. A large party of very gay ladies were up for the day from Southend. The party comic, a rather stout lady, came on the stage to compete in a musical quiz and before we even started she kept "goosing" me and after a few minutes of this she suddenly blurted out at the top of her voice: "Come on Charlie, giss me bleedin' prize and let's piss orf!"

How do you follow that?

Take Pot Luck was the only show of its kind to be invited to take part in the Scottish Radio and TV Exhibition at Kelvin Hall. For this I made it almost a three-ringed circus. I had several competitions going on at once and the finale was superb. I had rehearsed the whole vast audience singing *Road to the Isles* in hushed voices, while Marian Miller sang *My Ain Folk*, which somehow blended in harmony with a backcloth of the Edinburgh Castle. I had the George Mitchell singers and the Pipe Band all in a combination that proved to be very effective.

For this one show I decided that when in Scotland do as the Scottish do and I was measured for and kitted out with the kilt and dress uniform. Being theatrical I chose the Macbeth Tartan, not the most startling in colour, but very beautiful. It may sound trite, but although, strictly speaking, I was not entitled to wear the kilt, it gave me a sense of pride. The jabot, the lace, the flounces, the buckles and the skean dhu, the tiny dagger in the stocking. It is a flattering dress and indeed it made me realise how badly we English need a costume such as this. A national costume, something that can be worn with pride. Wales has one, the Scots, Luxembourg, Holland, Portugal, Spain and yet all we English can seem to muster as a national costume is a bowler hat and a rolled umbrella.

Perhaps if we did have some sort of national costume that could be worn, such as the kilt, our teenagers might wear it with some awareness. Who knows, it might even inspire a little more national pride!

It was St George's Day that set me off on an idea for radio. I have always been proud of my own birthright, and I've always enjoyed writing poetry. With these two factors I wrote a poem for St George's Day and it went down rather well. I then suggested that the listeners write either a poem of their own for St George's Day, or indeed any poem. It snowballed to such an extent that I have read some thousands of them over the air. The BBC published a collection of some entitled *A Bouquet of Verse*. It had this title because I send a bouquet of flowers to the writer of what, in my opinion, is the best of the month.

I don't know what inspired me to write poetry, but looking back, I think it was probably a one-armed pavement artist who used to sit by the Thames Embankment near Blackfriars Bridge. I was so moved by his workmanship that I wrote a poem about him.

It was Bud Flanagan who suggested that I should be called Poet Laureate of the Grand Order of Water Rats and I have been proud of the title since 1953. If one of our members should pass on, I write a short tribute which would be read out from behind the vacant chair in Lodge. These were beautifully copied and framed, but as time went by there were so many that they had to be put aside into the museum.

When "Olly" of Laurel and Hardy passed on, I penned one to his memory and Stan received a copy of it. Here is what he wrote to me from Malibu, California:

October 11th, 1957

My dear Charlie,

Have just received a copy of your wonderful eulogy to my dear late partner Olly, which Leonard Jones so kindly sent to me.

It is difficult for me Charlie to express my deep appreciation for your kind and sweet thought, in creating this beautiful tribute, but I want you to know I feel very grateful to you for the lovely sentiment. My sincere thanks Charlie. Am having it framed.

Trust all's well and happy with you, wish you continued success.

Bye, good luck and God bless,
Sincerely always
STAN
Stan Laurel

Alas I little realised that all too soon I was destined to write a similar eulogy to Stan. Two great gentlemen, who will remain a legend in the world of laughter.

I once composed a poem on sentry duty during the war and later it was the subject of a whole sermon by Bishop Chevasse of Rochester. The bishop became a friend of mine and whenever I played Chatham, or any town near, he would be in my dressing room saying: "Make me laugh Charlie, I haven't got long to live." He knew he had cancer, but I never saw him depressed.

I was also very friendly with Canon Freshwater in Blackpool. He always took the Actors' Service. His opposite number, the Reverend Tom Allcock came to my dressing room one day and chatted about religion. I gave him my points of view and he was so impressed at my argument that I was a Christian without a religion, he asked me to go to his pulpit on the following Sunday and, in lieu of a sermon, have the argument with him there.

I did, and we 'played' to a full house.

*

How the mind plays us tricks! We forget names and remember faces, or we remember names and forget faces. It often struck me as one of the odd factors of life that certain conversations or simple remarks can remain with us for ever, and yet whole subjects carefully and systematically drilled into us at school, are completely forgotten. Things we are often meant to remember, we choose not to retain, and yet some things best forgotten, we remember far too long.

It may have something to do with the impact on us at the time of utterance. I know that I shall never forget my Army number. I don't particularly want to remember it, it is of no use to me, yet the telephone numbers I want to remember keep evading me.

My mind recalls many simple little pleasures that will

never leave me, like the time I first met Alec (Funny Face) Pleon. He was a corporal in the Army. He had a yodelling act on stage in civilian life and having been a yodeller in my earlier days I had more than a passing interest in him.

We talked of show business and during the conversation I mentioned a yodelling act on my first variety bill – a man and wife. I hadn't heard of a woman yodeller before and she fascinated me. They were most kind to me and treated me like a son. I grew very fond of them both. Their name was Daimler and Edie.

Alec's face lit up. He said: "Thank you for that, I'm so pleased. Daimler and Edie are my mother and father."

On another occasion, when I was in *Boeing Boeing*, there was a young man playing opposite me who had to grow a beard which added a few years to him and made him more believable in the part. In the course of conversation in the dressing room, I mentioned something to him that I have already quoted earlier in this book, and that was about the fine actor called Ian Fraser. I was saying what a great artiste he was and generally praising his work, when the young man said: "Oh it's nice to hear you say that, he's my grandfather." No sooner had he said it than his grandfather walked in.

I do seem to hold on to my friends for a long time. It was in the S and S Club back in the late thirties that I met a charming girl, who was always "big" on any bill. The Club got it's name from the two famous men who ran it, Stanelli and Leslie Sarony. All the elite of show business went there and one of them was this young lady – Tessie O'Shea. She remains the same today, always effervescent and with all her successes, both here and in America, still retains that northern homeliness, which she will never lose.

Peggy Ryan, the amazing tap-dancing film star from America, who made such lovely films with Donald O'Connor, danced in my show *The Big Show of 1950* at the Palladium, with her new partner Ray Macdonald. We have written to each other since, and although her home is now in

Honolulu, there is a standing invitation for me to go there.

I also became a firm friend of Hollywood stars Forrest Tucker and Howard Keel. I remember Howard when he was touring this country. We were often playing "opposite" theatres and sharing the same hotel. He has a marvellous laugh and had a great feeling for comedy, and for me the singing and choreography in his film *Seven Brides for Seven Brothers* will be unequalled for a long time.

One of the great ladies of show business who became a legend, was Sophie Tucker. I first met her when she was using my dressing room for a Sunday show at Blackpool. I called to see her to pay my respects and in the little outer room was a trolley with the remains of tomato and chopped liver. I knocked and was invited in. I think I expected to see her done up in all her glory, instead there was this "Yiddisher Mamma" sitting there in an old dressing gown with a large pair of knee length bloomers washed out and hanging over the wash basin. A more ordinary woman you could not imagine, and yet, what magnetism. At first I thought she was going to be a little hostile to me.

"Hello. What do you want?" she asked.

"Oh excuse me, I've just called to see you. I'm Charlie Chester. I'm here for the season and this is my room!"

"So what do you want? *Rent?*"

I smiled, and after wishing her well I made as if to leave.

"What's your hurry then? Dontcha wanna talk to me?"

"Well yes, that was the idea."

"Well pull up a chair!"

I did, and we talked for almost an hour. She was all keyed up, not about her performance, but about the book she had written. She was anxious for it to do well, as the proceeds were going to the Jewish Relief Fund.

But we also talked of many other things and she told me about a new thing in the States called an 'electric razor'. I hadn't heard of such things at the time and she said: "Oh you must have one, I believe they are marvellous, I'll get you one."

209

Naturally I thanked her and expected her to forget it; she had bigger things on her mind. Several months later I had a phone call from the customs people at Southampton, saying that they were holding an electric razor sent over by Sophie Tucker. She didn't know my address or agent and thought the best thing to do was send it care of the Customs. Sophie was a Dame of the Grand Order of Lady Ratlings, and her generosity was only equalled by her great artistry. I shall always hold affection for my "Yiddisher Mamma".

Tommy Trinder has a frightening memory, but he remembers the times you would prefer to forget. We had a lot of fun together in Yarmouth, when he played at the Windmill for Jack and Freda Jay and I was at the Aquarium. Toni, Tommy's wife, used to enjoy flying a plane and she would fly with a trailer billowing out behind saying, COME TO THE TRINDER SHOW right over the queue at our box office. I couldn't "top" that.

At nights in the hotel, Tommy would test my memory to see just how far back I could remember. But one night, I decided to put his memory to the test; I was trying to recall the name of an act I worked with at the Prince of Wales.

"Tommy, you must remember his name . . . he used to do an act called a Cavalcade of Junk." Tommy searched his brain and shook his head. "You remember, he used to wear an enormous overcoat with giant pockets in and carry on a large leather bag, then he would take things out of his pockets like candlesticks and feather dusters and all kinds of junk and drop them into the bag."

Still no recognition.

"Thick set fellow, very untidy, used to drink a lot!"

Still nothing.

"A Cavalcade of Junk."

Another shake of the head.

Suddenly I thought of something. "He once had an affair with a red-headed usherette!"

Like a flash he said: "Oh you mean Ed Morelle."

My show finished one week earlier and at the end of our

210

run, a goldfish was handed up in a bowl with a message from Tommy saying. "This is so you won't feel too lonely in the Aquarium."

I promptly went out and bought a budgie in a cage and arranged for it to be handed up to him at his finale saying, "You can always admit you got the bird for churning out the corn at the Windmill."

Tommy loves a gag about himself. I once cracked one about him when he did the ice show. Norman Wisdom had done it the previous year and Tommy was tickled when I said: "It was a sign of the times – last year they had Wisdom on ice, this year they've got ignorance on it." I wouldn't have remembered this gag – it was Tommy who reminded me.

At the Marsden Hospital, Tommy stood behind me and kept whispering things in my ear. We were all standing around where Curly, Bud Flanagan's widow, was digging the spot for the foundation stone, and during the few words of reverence that were spoken, Tommy breathed quietly: "Danny La Rue would have been here today . . . only he's had a miscarriage!"

Tommy will always be regarded as one of the best comics in the business. He has a certain aggressiveness which hides his real self, and this aggressiveness comes out occasionally, but I think it does with most people who have been kicked around a bit.

There are few who can out talk Tommy, and he tells of an amusing exchange when he played two clubs in one night. The first, he went like a bomb, but in the second, the Levenshulme Sporting Club, they just wouldn't listen, the noise was dreadful. Tommy opened with his usual: "Trinders the name," and he might just as well have said "How do you do?" to an entire Wembley Stadium Cup Final crowd, the amount of notice they took. He tried again with the same result, and finally he said: "Well it's obvious that you don't want to know, and come to that, I don't particularly want to be here, so goodnight." With that, he stalked off the stage.

The entertainments manager grabbed him and said: "What do you think you're doing? You'll never play here again."

Tommy snapped: "Will you put that in writing?"

Tommy is, and always has been, a strict teetotaller. Something I admire him for, even though I don't agree with everything he says. I can remember asking him one day at Yarmouth Races, why he came, because he wouldn't watch the races, nor was he interested in having a bet.

"Horses were made for pulling carts!" was his remark, and that is something that I, naturally, disagree with.

On the subject of drink though, I have always been a little disturbed at the amount consumed by the lads in the forces when in outlying places. It's none of my business I know, but having seen them, young lads, in the bars and messes, just knocking them back, simply because there is nothing much else to do in spare time, and getting stoned, seems such a pity to me.

I saw the terrible result of a drinking bout in Korea when I visited a young man who was lying at death's door. He had been asleep in bed when his tent mate came back one night, drunk and out of his mind, and kicked the kerosene lamp and contents all over his sleeping mate. The man ran out like a flaming torch down the compound and finally collapsed. Whether he survived I don't know, but the incident would never have occurred if his tent mate had been sober.

I have explained earlier that I never drank until I was over forty, and then only to propose various toasts at functions where I had to speak. There is nothing nicer than to see a man or woman enjoy a drink, but there is nothing more disturbing than to see very young serving men trying to hold their end up with the others and drinking themselves stupid, night after night.

One of the most rewarding jobs and yet one of the most heart rending, is to entertain the war wounded. I have done this at so many places, and yet one place, and one man, sticks out in my mind as perhaps the most dreadful of all.

The place was called Hill End, just outside Edinburgh, and after touring the wards I was asked to go and cheer up one old chap. He was in a room all to himself. My eyes boggled at a chair on wheels which held a stump. Just a head and body, with no legs or arms. His medals were proudly pinned across his chest and held flat by the straps that held him there. How do you make such a man as that laugh? The living remains of a man made me want to weep anyway. Yet, laugh he did, loud and long. I came away thinking that if I hadn't a crust in this world, just to be able to walk away under my own steam made me the richest man in creation.

I will never become the richest man in the world but I think I can claim to be one of the friendliest. I can honestly say that I have never met a man I didn't want to like. I find, however, that some of them won't let you, and some you regret liking, but I have always wanted to be friends with everybody.

In America it's possible to create a feud verbally, and make it a very commercial gimmick. Bob Hope and Bing were most adept at friendly slanging. So, for that matter, were Dorothy Parker and Dorothy Thompson, only theirs was not quite so friendly. The one I worked up with Henry Hall had to be dropped because the listening audience liked us both and couldn't quite understand why we got at each other.

The most spiteful pair were George Formby and Max Miller. When George went over to entertain the British Expeditionary Force, he sent a message back that some stars playing the relative comforts of the London Palladium should offer their services and go "over there".

Miller took umbrage at this and replied: "I did go 'over there' in 1914, but I carried a rifle, not a ukelele!"

One of the most tumultuous receptions I ever remember, was actually before the show started. It was in Brussels, three days after the liberation. My small company of soldier entertainers were to perform the first show there as an allied performance. The first half of the bill were 'Continental' acts, mostly Belgian and French. We were to do the entire second half. The audience were fifty per cent Allied troops and fifty per cent French and Belgian civilians.

As it was the first show after the liberation I had an idea. In the intermission following the Continental acts, I had all the lights put out, even those in the exit boxes. This meant that the place was in complete darkness, and just before the second half was due to begin, suddenly, in the pitch black auditorium, all that could be heard was the semaphore signal for V̇ sounded on the tympany drum. This was the BBC signal to the freedom fighters promising victory. As soon as the continentals heard it in the darkness the place erupted into the greatest ovation I have ever heard. It was a proud moment.

Even a seasoned performer can be shaken at times, and I think one of the most disturbing moments for me was during a TV show for the American Forces at Prestwick airfield long after the war was over.

I don't know how, or why, but the time of recording and transmission was altered and I assumed that all the performers had been told. I was ready to open the show, and so were the girls, so I had no reason to think that everyone else wasn't ready. The girls opened to a roar from the Americans, then I went on, and with gags like: "I know you guys are well paid, I saw the money arrive by Wells Fargo!" This was only a preliminary gag before announcing the act that would set them alight: Don Lang and the Frantic Five. I led into my announcement, gave him the build up, shouted his name and suddenly someone in the wings whispered: They're still in the village shopping!"

I thought "Oh God, I can't hold the fort that long", but I launched into a routine about Marilyn Monroe, and a couple of bosom gags had the American lads laughing. We switched an act quickly, and Don was back with his lads in time to do his act. Somehow he hadn't been told of the change of plans, and thinking back, Marilyn's bosoms were a real couple of pals to me on that occasion.

Probably the best young fan I had was a little lad called

Louis, at Southsea. He came to the pantomime and sat in the gallery no less than twenty-seven times. I use a baby white rabbit as a running gimmick in panto, and he called round to the stage door with carrots. It was then that I learned of the number of times he had been. He told me that he was bringing his sister and elder brother the next time. I invited them all to supper with me, telling him to ask his mother if it was all right. Instead of the little urchin he usually looked, he was all smartened up, and explaining what hors d'oeuvres meant, was hilarious to say the least. This little chap won my heart completely and he came so often, we used to pause at certain tag lines in the school sketch and shout up to the gallery for him to say the line. He broke his heart when we left, and I must admit that I was sad too. But he did write to me several times and although his letters eventually stopped, I shall always remember little Louis.

You have probably gathered that I am very fond of children, but there are some who can incite murder.

The best example of this was on the occasion I bought a new Buick. It was a long, blue, sleek, left-hand drive car, that attracted a lot of attention. I left it outside Stan Matthews place, then before going in I remembered I wanted a particular magazine, so I walked down to the newsagents. Having bought the paper I retraced my steps to the house and then suddenly, to my horror, a little kid with a bucket and spade, walked along by the side of the gleaming monster, and for no earthly rhyme or reason, was going to bash the front mudguard with his spade.

I paled. I was rooted to the spot. I was quickly totting up in my mind the cost of a new respray. The mother rushed forward and I heard her shout as she shook him: "Don't you dare . . . that's a brand new *spade*!"

I don't know which I wanted to kill, the kid, or the mother.

Delights of the flesh can come fairly easy to a star name on tour. Young girls can also be a danger, for they tend to hide their real age, or rather their real youth.

When I first went to Liverpool Empire, I had an enormous crowd at the stage door for autographs, and the first to confront me were four young girls. I signed their books and joined in their banter. Instead of going away afterwards, however, they stayed until I had signed the rest. I was now left with these four young lasses, and their leader said quietly: "Where are you staying Charlie?"

"The Adelphi," I told her.

Then she leaned forward and said confidentially: "If you book us in, you can have all four of us!" I gagged my way out of the situation and realised the seriousness of it; these girls couldn't have been a day older than fifteen!

I always had a great deal of mail waiting for me at theatres while I was on tour. I opened one letter which moved me greatly. It was from an old age pensioner, enclosing pension book, identity card and other documents. The letter was asking me to buy him a new pair of boots.

I knew I couldn't possibly purchase boots for anyone not knowing the size, and besides they are such a personal thing only the wearer can do it. I therefore sent money instead and returned the documents.

Two weeks later, I received the same letter at a different theatre and I realised when I received it for the third time, that it was a glorious 'con' trick.

I have to smile when I think of the tricks of our own profession, and one incident in particular. It concerned trick lighting with ultra violet lights, and an act called Dumarte and Denza. These people wore skin tights of black with skeleton bones painted on them. When the lighting came into effect all that could be seen were the dancing skeletons. Various tricks could be employed, such as removing a head so that it danced separately to the body, and so on. It was a very effective act and usually brought the house down.

It was not uncommon for them to also employ any dancers which happened to be on the bill, to swell the numbers of skeletons. One of the acts on the bill while we

216

were on tour in a rural area of Cornwall, was Ray and Jackie Penn, two young tap dancers. They were employed as a couple of skeletons with Dumarte and Denza. The yokels were absolutely fascinated, but when the skeletons ran out into the audience and up the gangway, one old farmer was so unconvinced he shouted: "I don't believe it," and promptly kicked out at a skeleton. Poor Ray Penn, he was the one who stopped the boot and broke his ankle.

A lot is made these days of overweight and slimming, but just after the war, on my first tour, I had a French act called the Monna Tymga Four. This consisted of the father of two strapping lads and a young French girl. It was an adagio act, where the two giant lads would throw the girl across the stage and she would be caught by the senior member.

Having been deprived of good food during the war years, the young lady had developed an appetite for steaks, even horse steaks, which were then on the menu. I have known her eat a whole meal and then order the same again. Not surprisingly she slowly became heavier. One night, it manifested itself to such an extent that when the boys threw her across the stage in a kind of swallow dive, the old man caught her and the weight of her knocked him backwards and they fell in a heap.

The finale of the first half was a jungle scene in which I did a comedy routine dance with Arthur Haynes – me as the girl, and Arthur as the cave man. George Black had an idea to bring up the applause, and that was to build up the finale with everybody coming on and taking up their positions. I was to be lifted by one leg by the French boys, held high at arm's length, and walked on in an artistic pose. This was fine, except that as most men, I possess fairly long, fine hairs on my thighs, and as the giant hands held my weight by the one leg, the resin on their hands was naturally pulling all the hairs out slowly! As if this were not enough to contend with the strong man's thumb was even more disconcerting, and I could do nothing about it!

217

If there was one thing that George and Alfred Black specialised in, it was stage presentation. They knew how to build a scene up and up so that the applause snowballed into a crescendo. To this end they always had a fine producer and designer. Alec Shanks would build a miniature stage in cardboard and each scene would be made scaled down. The dresses for the show ladies were all drawn with great artistry and colour. He would sit in the auditorium throughout the rehearsals and have a microphone, through which he would shout instructions to the lighting men over the music. It was all a very serious business.

The finale was the big scene. Drums were the theme – drums large and small, with keyboards and drums going back into infinity. They even had the programme sellers as drum majorettes.

At the end of the first performance Alec went to the back of the theatre, to try and hear any comments about the show as the people went out. He tells me that after all the work he put into his idea of the drum scene, he could have gladly strangled the little lady who said: "It were loovely . . . eee and I *did* enjoy the hat-box scene!"

There is one scene, however, that almost makes me sick when I think of it, and that wasn't on a stage, it was after a show.

I was in a farce called *Done in Oils*, a very funny show we performed in Hull. The young actors and actresses in the show were all broke and there was snow everywhere and they were all grateful when I suggested that I treat them to a fried fish supper. The smell of it was gorgeous as we approached the little shop. After I had ordered and the fish and chips were being wrapped in newspaper, I asked if we could go into the back room and eat it. I quite thought that there was a place to do so.

"Yes, go in by all means, just through the door."

We trooped in holding our hot packages, and suddenly found ourselves, not in a room with tables to sit at, but confronting us was an enormous sink that took up the

218

greater part of a cubby-hole. In it, and all over the floor, were all the dead heads from the fish. It was a ghastly sight, but the company was too hungry to care. They dipped into their meals with their fingers and ate the lot.

*

Entertaining in prisons is both amusing and sad.

They are a first-class audience and for a comic they are superb. I didn't know the jargon for warders when I first arrived, and when I tripped on a floorboard as I went on stage, I looked up and one of the screws holding it down was raised. I said: "Oh pardon me, I've just tripped over a screw!" The place fell in, and it wasn't until afterwards, I learned that 'screw' is the inmates' name for a warder. My next big laugh came when I said: "It's bloody draughty standing here; has someone left a door open?"

I was fascinated by the men who wore yellow patches on their clothes. These were the men who had tried to escape, and in one prison, the governor showed me some of their handiwork – keys, dozens and dozens of them. They try to memorise the pattern of the big master key, and with an ordinary Gillette razor handle they cut out a small channel, and then insert two patterned pieces of brass into the channel. It may only work the once and then fall to pieces, but once, if it works, is all that is necessary. The Governor told me of one man who was searched every fifteen minutes, and *still* he made keys!

From bad boys to good girls brings me to the Rodney Hudson Troupe of girls who were to entertain at a cabaret function. Ronald Frankau went on to do a routine and then introduced the girls: "And now ladies and gentlemen, we come to a delightful group of dancers, may I now introduce to you Mrs Rodney Hudson's Eight Virgins!"

As he walked off, old Ma Hudson was purple with rage. "How dare you say that about my girls." she spluttered.

Ronald turned about and walked back on stage and said:

"I'm sorry ladies and gentlemen, I understand they are *not* virgins!"

I'm a sentimental old fool in many ways, and for years I have always signed my autograph with a kiss. I don't do this magnanimously, but because of an event that occurred outside the stage door of the London Palladium. After the second performance one night, I was on my way home and outside, standing in the pouring rain were two women. One approached me and I asked why they were standing out there in the rain. The younger of the two, who herself must have been seventy, said: "We saw the first show and we've been waiting here ever since. You see my friend is blind, and she's ninety. She's heard you on the radio so much, and she has no family of her own, so she wondered if you would kiss her goodnight."

I not only kissed her goodnight, I took her home, and because of that old lady I always sign my name with a kiss.

Mind you, it hasn't been love and kisses all the way. There were times when I wondered what I had done wrong. For instance, notwithstanding the thousands of broadcasts and series I had done over the years on radio and TV since the retirement of my producer Leslie Bridgmont, I was never again offered my own comedy radio series. I have been in many radio shows, and more recently in a comedy programme called *The Gag Crackers Ball*, produced by John Fawcett Wilson, but the Charlie Chester crazy comedy shows seemed to be at an end. At one time, I was deeply frustrated when the only two comedy scripted shows were headed by the two straight men of the business. Kenneth Horne, who did an amazingly funny show called *Round the Horne*, and Nicholas Parsons.

I went over to record shows. *Housewives' Choice* to begin with. Then, when Tom Sloane became the boss of TV things began to change. I had been good friends with Tom when he was second in command to two previous heads, and at a lunch in White City, he told me that he intended to make a few changes. He didn't tell me what though. I was just finishing my current series of *Take Pot Luck*, and I was awarded the "Bucket".

The "Bucket" was, in effect, one of the huge copper and brass humidors which are placed by the lifts and at various other vantage points. When Victor Borge proved such a sensation and they wanted to make him a gift, they asked what he would like. He pointed to the large ash-tray bucket and said: "I'd like one of those." So a plaque of brass was appended and it was presented to him. This became the "Popularity Award" at Television Centre.

When they did my *This Is Your Life*, I was then awarded the "Bucket" and before I could say "knife" the door shut. I wasn't invited back to do anything on TV which had almost been my home, for years.

I submitted seven different show ideas to Tom. He returned them all. Strange how it all happened so suddenly, no comedy radio shows, and now no TV. I did some appearances. There was always summer season and panto-mime, but my first loves had disappeared.

I wrote children's books to fill in some of my time. Later I recorded them for Pye Records, with classical music to background the stories. Although the books won the accolade of the Hanover Book Fair, the lovely Katie Boyle, writing for a magazine, slated the records.

Kate, is quite a character, and although the epitome of an English beauty, is Italian by birth. We were once on a TV panel in Weymouth, and she asked if I was motoring back to London after the show, I told her that I was, and she decided to come back with me. As she was going from "door to door" so to speak, she decided not to change her clothes and stepped into my Rolls in a full evening gown, looking a delight.

On leaving the precincts of the town, we smelled fish and chips, and Katie's blue eyes twinkled as she said: "Cor, do you smell that?"

"Want some?"

"Rather."

I stopped the car and backed up into a small opening leading to the fish shop, left Katie in the car and went in. As we had just been on TV they recognised me immediately and made the usual fuss. "Is that Katie Boyle in the car?" they asked. I told them it was, and before we knew it, there we were, me in evening dress, and Katie in black and gold *lamé* evening gown, eating fish and chips from a paper in the Rolls Royce, with half the community gathered around to watch us.

About this time I turned my attention to writing murder novels, all the while wanting to get back to radio and TV, and with this in mind I devised a show which finally had the title, *I Object*. It was an amusing idea with a difference. The format was that people would be invited to enter the witness box in a courtroom scene, with twelve people from the audience as the jury. Jimmy Edwards would be the judge, and Ted Ray and I would be the counsels for prosecution and defence. The plaintiff would then bring her complaint to the cameras, saying such things as: "I Object to my husband squeezing the toothpaste from the middle, when it should be done from the bottom." The prosecution would then try to prove that she had a legitimate grumble, whilst the other counsel would try to prove otherwise.

Frank Muir was head of comedy scripts at the time and although he had presented two shows, neither of them had clicked. He called me in and said it was the funniest idea that had been brought to him so far. I was delighted. Then, in a rather uncomfortable half hour, he asked me if I would withdraw from the show!

I was dumbfounded. Why?

He tried to explain that Ted Ray and Jimmy had been working on *Does the Team Think* for about twelve years and that they 'sparked' each other off. I asked him how he knew I wouldn't.

Next it was suggested that they wanted to put a real advocate in the show, and I knew that the same as doctors, this was not possible anyway. After that, it was a straight actor they wanted. All in all I could see that they wanted the vehicle, but not me.

I told Frank to forget the whole thing. I know he was rather cross with me for insisting that I wanted to appear in my own vehicle, and my argument went "upstairs". But poor Jimmy and Ted, together with myself, had to almost give an audition. We had to do a performance in an empty room at Broadcasting House, which was like ringing the death knell of a comedy vehicle before it even started.

I somehow think it was to prove that I might not fit in with the lads. However, it took the air on TV and ran for twelve weeks. I still think it could have run much longer, and after all that, we did have fun anyway.

About this time, my agent was rather cool. After being with him for twenty-two years, suddenly all his interest was centred on a new comedian and he appeared to have no further time for me. In fact, come to think of it, after twenty-two years, he never even said "Goodbye".

*The safest place to live, is just
inside your income.*

CHAPTER TEN

We have no right to happiness
without producing at least some of it.

IT appeared to me that the reason why programmes like
Housewives' Choice, which ran for about twenty years, were
so successful, was because it extended an invitation to the
public to write letters. I noticed too that columns of letters in
newspapers were now becoming half pages. They even got
to the point where they invited the public to "phone a
letter". A great number of these letters were full of wit, and
scathing comments, together with some very wise hints and
so on.

To me this was a "perfect radio" idea. Letters on certain
subjects both serious and humorous, could be followed by a
record applicable to the subject matter, and a couple of
cryptic asides from me was all that was necessary.

Little did I know what I had started.

Although it took me four years to sell the idea as a

programme, within a matter of weeks it had snowballed so much that I was receiving hundreds of letters weekly. It stays now at around the thousand-a-week mark, and the programme is now in its fifth year.

It's funny how, as a performer writer, you can devise and plug what you think is a good catch phrase, until it becomes a national remark such as "Can I do yer now sir?" in *ITMA*, or from my own shows *Whippit Kwick*, and "Don't force it Phoebe!" or "Whatcher Tish, Whatcher Tosh", and yet they are not always the ones to hit the mark. I remember that one of these catch phrases happened simply because of a joke I pulled on my wife. She had a broken arm in plaster and was sitting in the audience of a broadcast show. I told Len Marten to keep coming up to me and saying: "I say . . . what a smasher!" This was resolved after several times of repeating when I said: "What do you mean?" He nudged me and then said: "The blonde in the second row . . . I say, what a smasher."

As soon as the audience saw the plastered arm and realised we were pulling her leg they laughed. The following day, and for months after, people all over the country were saying: "I say! What a smasher."

This was one instance where it wasn't really meant to be a catch phrase, only a simple private little joke, but it happened.

In the same way, with my present show, things really developed, and it began to take on a shape much different to what I had originally envisaged.

As a pay-off I said something like: "Well there we are, dear friends, both home and overseas . . ." and this simple remark brought, and still brings me many letters from folks who have married someone from abroad and gone there to live.

Germany, France, Holland, Sweden, Norway – I have even had letters from Spain and Czechoslovakia. They all say in effect that the message made them feel that I was talking to them in particular and that it made them feel "at home".

One letter which began to change the whole concept of the programme came from Bristol. It was from a woman who explained that her husband was blind and badly handi-capped. She went on to tell me that because of this, he could do little but sit in a chair and wait for her to come home from work. "I can't afford a typewriter," she said, "but if only he had one, it would help him to fill in the waiting hours, and make a new life for him."

This made me think that there were probably hundreds of old typewriters, still useable, just collecting dust in attics and cellars. I appealed for a typewriter and read her letter over the air.

Almost by return of post, I was inundated with offers. One firm of opticians near the BBC offered me no less than forty-four from their branches all over the country, ranging from the north of Scotland to the south coast. This posed a problem for me, for now, they had to be collected and delivered. I remembered a wonderful organisation called Lions International. This is a world-wide organisation, made up of multiple districts, represented by individual clubs. They are chartered, and good, honest-to-God working men with a Christian approach to life, who have regular meetings to render what aid they can to the less privileged.

There are about a million and a half Lions in the world, and I am proud to be one of them, and these are represented by about 68,000 clubs. The fact that they are international means that they are able to help in many ways. To give an example of this, I first heard of the Lions through an achievement which made me marvel, both at its complexity and sincerity.

An old lady, nearing her eighties, happened to mention that she had a son in Australia, and knowing that she could never afford the fare, doubted that she would ever see her son again. Somehow this got to the ears of a Lion, and in consequence, without the dear lady's knowledge, this is what happened.

It was arranged that her fare would be paid, her son would be advised that she would be coming and, this is the best part, she was escorted to the plane by a Lion, and at every stopping place in the various countries, a Lion met her to make sure she was alright. A Lion met her in Australia and escorted her to her son, she enjoyed a wonderful stay, and the same process of escorts was arranged for her return journey.

If this was 'Lionism' then I was all for it. They accepted me in their ranks, and I have been a member ever since. Through the Lions clubs I have managed to collect and deliver from generous donors to delighted receivers, some four hundred and twenty-eight typewriters. Mostly to the blind and handicapped.

But it didn't stop at typewriters, before I knew it, soon peoples' generosity extended to radio sets, television sets, arm chairs, ambulances, wool for old folks for knitting, used stamps, trading stamps, spectacles for Zambia and clothes for the very poor.

The Grand Order of Water Rats, not to be outdone, have donated some dozens of Lord Snowdon chairmobiles for those unable to walk. Round table and rotary clubs, have also come in on the scheme. The Loyal Order of Moose and individual clubs and people, far too many to mention, have all offered their services. Without these I wouldn't be able to do the transportation jobs, and I have been deeply touched at their willingness to help.

Of course, it's not only the clubs I have mentioned who help out, there are certain individuals who have been so keen to help their fellow men that they have formed 'soapbox clubs' in various parts of the country. These keep me informed of what they are doing, and also tell me of certain articles and projects which are needed.

The one thing paramount to me is that people's generosity should not be abused, or handed out willy nilly. This is where my Lion associates are so very helpful, for they go and diplomatically "interview" to make sure that the case is genuine. If it is, they not only carry out the necessary task, but often take the people concerned under their wing and make periodical calls to see that all is well. In the five years that I have been operating this way, we have only had two professional scroungers.

Individuals have really amazed me with their generosity and I couldn't begin to list them all, but there are some that stand out in my mind. One was a patient in Broadmoor, who had heard my appeal regarding typewriters and he bought three brand new portables, together with paper and had them sent to me for distribution to two particular people.

One of them, believe it or not, was a woman with no hands! She sent me a typewritten letter, on a rather beaten up old typewriter, saying that she had a lot of work to do, but that she needed a typewriter. She typed with her feet. On delivering to her the new one purchased by the gentleman in Broadmoor, I asked her to show me how she did it.

Quite apart from doing a professional job, she was fascinating to watch. The hardest job for her is inserting the paper into the roller with her toes. However, she is quite independent about it and proceeds to pick up a stub of wood like a thick pencil, between her big toe and the next, and then taps the keys with this wooden stump. A truly amazing woman, and to see the joy of receiving her new typewriter was a pleasure I shall always remember.

One of the most amazing appeals, came from a woman in this country on behalf of her pen friend in the Phillipines. She wrote to me saying "I enclose herewith a letter from Lily Roma Robbins, it is self explanatory and Charlie, you were the only one I could think of."

The letter read ... "Please can you find me a benefactor? My husband, a leper, died on May 13th, leaving me with eight healthy children to feed, clothe and educate, and as an ex-leper, no one will employ me. I am destitute. Can you find me a benefactor?"

I sent the letter to International Lions HQ asking if they would consider meeting the challenge. Within three days, there was a meeting in Cebu City, and within three weeks, it was resolved.

What an achievement! All because of a band of men who have a great respect for each other and a great compassion for their fellow beings.

Each Sunday I ask for certain things, and it amazes me that practically everything I do ask for, is offered.

When I read a particularly sad letter, one lady, who wished to remain anonymous, sent me a blank cheque, and asked me to fill in the amount. I was overwhelmed with such complete trust, and so too were the firm with which I dealt, that I was sold the article at less than cost price.

One of the happiest moments came when I read a letter out from the grandmother of Samantha, a little girl with a hole in the heart, who longed for a pony. I immediately received a letter from a generous family in North Wales saying they had a little pony "Blackie" which they would gladly give to the little girl. Not only was the little pony given, but other kind people made a 500-mile round trip to collect and deliver it. I am happy to say that the little girl has survived two major heart operations and is now on the road to recovery.

On another occasion, an old ex-serviceman, fell asleep listening to his transistor in the park at Liverpool and it was stolen while he was asleep. He wrote and told me of his loss and that he could ill afford another, and I broadcast an appeal for an old transistor in the Liverpool area for this old soldier. By return came a cheque from a lady to purchase a new one for him.

Someone wrote on behalf of yet another old soldier, explaining that he was an ex-Desert Rat, ex-Royal Artillery – in fact an old soldier who had been through the wars in more ways than one, for he had recently undergone a major heart operation and was in a pretty bad way. He longed for a television set to occupy his lonely hours. I appealed for an unwanted set whereupon a colonel who wished to remain anonymous, wrote from Harrogate enclosing a cheque saying: "Don't give the old soldier a second-hand television set, buy him a new one."

One of the fastest deliveries was made to an old couple in Tunbridge Wells, Kent. This pair of pensioners longed for an old-type wind-up gramophone, that they could carry from room to room and play their old records. A gentleman from Catford heard the appeal and phoned to say that he had such a gramophone and that he was actually going down to Tunbridge Wells that evening. I came off the air at six o'clock. It was delivered to the old pair at eight!

When I asked for a record of *Home Sweet Home* for a old lady in Holland, I was inundated with them.

Of course there are the usual "try ons". I had one request from a "handicapped widow" for a transistor, who said hers was broken and she couldn't afford a new one. A simple enquiry revealed that she was not hard up at all, but just the reverse – she was the local prostitute

On another occasion, I had a desperate appeal for a TV set, but when the Lions called they discovered that the family were in no financial difficulties at all, and the "sick" gentleman who needed the TV set was out at a football match.

Of course it would be wrong to say that we manage to get everything we ask for; we never did get any replies for a "six foot stone Nun!" And there was a stony silence from me to the woman who wrote asking if I could lend her £50,000. She had it all worked out that with it she would buy a boarding house and put it in my name, so that when she died it would be mine anyway, so I couldn't lose! This made an earlier request for a loan of £30,000 seem very small!

Quite a number of the donated TV sets, naturally need

repair and attention, and to this end, we even have a young man in Abbey Wood, who repairs them for the needy – I emphasise – free of charge.

There was another man who heard my appeal for toys for children suffering from brain damage. He not only made five rocking horses – and beautifully made they were too – but loaded them aboard his car, and delivered them to my house for delivery to Margate.

One lady, hearing yet another appeal from me, drove all through the night to deliver an eiderdown, plus a hamper to an old lady in Northampton. It wasn't until after the event that I discovered the kind soul in question happened to be pianist of my very first concert party.

We were once inundated with requests after an appeal for a home for a neutered goat!

At the time of writing, I have just received a happy letter from a woman, who asked me to try and trace her long lost sister. Not only did we find the sister she had only met once, but also a brother whom she had never met at all.

From week to week therefore, with all these variations, life is not exactly dull, and even in this world of TV the old steam radio is still a powerful medium. It certainly has advanced in technique, but with nearly forty years experience at the mike I am still glad to be a part of it.

There is always something new, and nowadays, what with stereophonic sound, and quadrophonic sound, and synthesizers and the like, it never ceases to be interesting.

Whatever the new sounds and gimmicks though, whatever the new inventions and improvements, radio will always need people and their voices. Some of them please, others simply infuriate and I don't doubt that I do the same to many but I have always tried to win my way through the ear, to the heart.

From Charlie Chan to Charlie Chaplin, from Charlie Peace to Charlie McCarthy, and with our own Prince Charles admitting that he signs himself in at one particular club as Charlie Chester (which, as the Earl of Chester, he is quite entitled to do), it does seem that *The World Is Full of Charlies*, and on reflection, I don't think I would want to change places with any one of them.

> *Remember that there is no rebate to life,*
> *Not for one single moment you live,*
> *So why not enjoy, what there is to enjoy?*
> *And forgive . . . what there is, to forgive.*